PLATE I.

The Feast after a Hunt

TRAITS OF
AMERICAN INDIAN LIFE
AND CHARACTER

Attributed to

PETER SKEENE OGDEN

DOVER PUBLICATIONS, INC.
NEW YORK

Published in Canada by General Publishing Company, Ltd., 30 Lesmill Road, Don Mills, Toronto, Ontario.

Published in the United Kingdom by Constable and Company, Ltd., 3 The Lanchesters, 162–164 Fulham Palace Road, London W6 9ER.

Bibliographical Note

This Dover edition, first published in 1995, is an unabridged republication of the work originally published in 1933, as Rare Americana Series Number Nine, by The Grabhorn Press, San Francisco, where authorship was "By a Fur Trader." Illustrations and type were originally in two colors.

Library of Congress Cataloging-in-Publication Data

Ogden, Peter Skene, 1790–1854.
    [Traits of American Indian life & character]
    Traits of American Indian life and character / attributed to Peter Skeene Ogden.
        p.   cm.
    Originally published: Traits of American Indian life & character / by a Fur trader. London : Smith, Elder, 1853.
    ISBN 0-486-28436-0 (pbk.)
    1. Indians of North America—Washington (State)   2. Indians of North America—Oregon.   3. Indians of North America—Social life and customs. I. Title.
E78.W3032   1995
970.004'97—dc20
                                       94-33527
                                       CIP

Manufactured in the United States of America
Dover Publications, Inc., 31 East 2nd Street, Mineola, N.Y. 11501

Preface

MODESTLY *cloaking himself in anonymity, "A Fur Trader" has given us intimate sketches of the Far West savage, his life and his contacts with the roving trapper of which even Fenimore Cooper would have been proud to acknowledge the authorship. Authentic reports of the decade from 1830 to 1840 descriptive of the American Indian west of the Rockies are few; yet among those few this book—believed to have been written by Peter Skeene Ogden, one of the Hudson's Bay Company's most esteemed servants—stands forth.*

To "A Fur Trader's" text, illustrations made at the period he covers, have been added. The original edition published in London in 1853 was issued without plates. Otherwise no changes have been made.

The Grabhorn Press in publishing Traits of American Indian Life *as Number 9 of its Series of Rare Americana truly feels that it is not only preserving a valuable and little known work but that it is providing its readers with an intensely interesting book which covers a subject and a period of our national life but slightly touched upon by historians and writers.*

Douglas S. Watson, *Editor*

CONTENTS

ILLUSTRATIONS

from Father De Smet's Missions de l'Oregon et Voyages aux Montagnes Rocheuses, *Gand,* 1848

TO

LADY SIMPSON,

THE FOLLOWING SKETCHES AND ANECDOTES

ILLUSTRATIVE OF LIFE

ON THE WILD BORDERS OF THE PACIFIC, AND OF THE

SAVAGE TRIBES HOLDING INTERCOURSE WITH THE

HONOURABLE HUDSON'S BAY COMPANY,

OVER WHICH

SIR GEORGE SIMPSON

HAS SO LONG AND SO ABLY PRESIDED,

ARE DEDICATED,

AS A SMALL

TRIBUTE OF AFFECTIONATE REGARD,

BY HER LADYSHIP'S SINCERE AND DEVOTED FRIEND,

THE AUTHOR.

Introduction

IT is well known that the life of an Indian trader is one of hazard and adventure; and that he is the witness of scenes, exemplifying the habits and the character of Indians, which it is seldom the lot of an ordinary traveller to look upon. Compelled to penetrate the wilderness, hundreds of miles beyond the resort of civilized men, he surprises the savage inhabitants in their most secluded haunts, and often makes himself a home where the keenness of his observation, his previous knowledge of character, and the material interests of the wild race by which he is surrounded, are the only pledges of his safety. The long established trading posts also, in the neighbourhood of which some degree of civilization may obtain, are lone and isolated spots, the light of which dimly fades away in the surrounding darkness, and but too often brings into strong relief, on its confines, the startling forms and hideous characteristics of a barbaric life, which is yet gilded with some traits of nobleness and generosity, and which the trader, if any man living, is enabled to look upon with an intelligent eye.

Such are the circumstances and such the situation in which the writer of the following pages has been placed, as an agent of the great trading Company whose operations now cover as with a vast network the breast of the North American continent, from Hudson's Bay to the Pacific Ocean.

Introduction

As an actor in the scenes which he has faithfully described, it is just possible that he may sometimes express his opinions with unusual warmth. His sincerity, and the fidelity of his narrations, no one will doubt, when they find the savage virtues as conspicuous in many of his sketches as the darker traits of character which it was his more especial purpose to delineate.

The shifting scene of his narrative may be described, for the most part, as the famous Oregon territory, lying in the watercourse of the great Columbia River and its numerous tributaries. The country is one of wild aspect, diversified by rugged steeps and deep ravines, with here and there a rich valley of green pasture, watered by some mountain torrent pursuing its devious way to the broad waters and boundless prairie lands, or sandy plains. The wild races inhabiting this widely-spread region are of various character; in general, those who follow the chase—the mountain and woodland tribes — are the more warlike and generous; while those who live along the banks of the streams in the more fertile regions, are comparatively mean in spirit and treacherous in their intercourse. To this rule, it may be observed, there are many exceptions on the east side of the Rocky Mountains, which it is scarcely necessary to mention.

If the author can be said to have any preference for one of these swarthy clans before another, it is possibly for the chivalrous "Flatheads," who "have never been known to shed the blood of a white man," and are as brave in war as the "Crows" and "Blackfeet," their hereditary enemies. *It is against these latter, more especially, that his righteous anathemas are hurled as the persecutors of the Indian trader, whose courage and hardihood often avail nothing, when beset by Indians in the defiles of the mountains, or threading his way through the mazes of the forest. To surprise the weary traveller in the security of his sleep, to attack the camp in some luckless moment when discipline is for a while relaxed; or, least*

Five different tribes, inhabiting the plain country to the east of the Rocky, are denominated Blackfeet, viz., Piegans, Blood Indians, "Gros Ventres" or Big Bellies, Surcies, and Blackfeet Proper.

Introduction

of all, to rob the armed traders and trappers of their stray pack-horses, these predatory bands will follow them through wood and ravine for weary days and nights, lurking with untiring patience in the bushes, like beasts of prey, or peering from the crevices of the rocks till the yell of their sudden onset renders concealment no longer possible or necessary.

The traits of Indian life and character illustrated by the following sketches are, however, not all, nor even for the most part, of this nature; some of them are domestic scenes of tragic interest, and others relate occurrences in which the Indians had little or no direct share. It may be observed here, also, that great and rapid changes are taking place, by which the native population of these wilds is more sensibly affected every succeeding year. Not the least of these is the extended organization of the great Fur Company, which has now penetrated the remotest districts, and sends its emissaries into the most secluded glens. Next to this, perhaps, may be reckoned the rivalry of the English and American adventurers, and the recent influx of immigrants from the United States.

A word on this subject, on the toils and privations which must necessarily be undergone by those who seek a home beyond the Rocky Mountains, may not be out place. It is hard to conceive by what inducement so many thousands of reasonable men could have been prevailed on to leave their comfortable homes and fertile lands for this wild adventure; except, indeed, the spirit of enterprise, which seems to be inherent in the Anglo-American race, and which rejoices to meet and overcome every kind of difficulty, is sufficient to account for it. By whatever hope induced to undertake this distant pilgrimage, it is sad to think of the disappointment that awaits the lately happy family whose homestead is broken up, and their little all conveyed into these deserts by the poor animals which had heretofore rendered such useful service on their farms;—sad to picture them, herding together for mutual protection, as they advance slowly, while the months roll on, through a country teeming with warlike ma-

Introduction

rauders, and often surprised by the treacherous bands described in these pages. In course of time the waters of the Missouri roll behind them, and the river of their hopes may be seen glancing in the distance. Now, however, the dreary wastes of burning sand and scrubby wormwood, unrelieved by any nobler vegetation and affording a scanty pasture to the tired quadrupeds at wide intervals only, begin to dissipate the sanguine hopes in which they had so lately indulged. Provisions fail; hunger, thirst, privation in every form are endured; till, weary and way-worn, the travellers at length reach the banks of the Columbia. If fortunate, they effect various exchanges with the Indians for fresh horses, to replace their own tired animals no longer able to proceed. Their little hoards of ready money are expended to procure the necessaries of existence, and they arrive at length in the settlements denuded of everything — in short, destitute — to begin the world anew.

While the hazards these adventurers must undergo, and the savage life of the wilderness for which they are bound, will be found illustrated in these occasional sketches of Indian life, it may be well to remark that to depict them has not been the object of the author; as the occurrences he has described were spread over many years, and have a different kind of interest. Impressed by them at the time as an eye-witness, he has here recorded them without art or ornament, in the hope that they may serve for the amusement of others who feel an interest in tales of adventure, and to add to the stock of authentic anecdotes from which alone a true judgment of the Indian character can be formed.

PLATE II.

The Scout Discovers the Herd

CHAPTER I.

Experience of the Indian Character

HAVING had frequent opportunities of observing the customs and traits of character by which the various tribes of Indians are distinguished, and more particularly of those who inhabit the western part of North America beyond the Rocky Mountains, I have been surprised to remark how falsely their character is estimated in the recently published journals of certain travellers. These gentlemen have been delighted to represent the aborigines of North America, as quiet, peaceable souls, meriting nothing so much as the most delicate attention on the part of their European visitors. Two works of this description are more particularly in my mind at this moment. The author of the first, it is to be observed, scarcely left the confines of civilization; and the second had merely an opportunity of communicating with a few Indians who had resided from their infancy in the vicinity of long established trading posts, where they had acquired the art of comporting themselves with some degree of propriety, in order the more readily to gain a livelihood and to acquire the means of satisfying their fictitious wants. The forefathers of these people, being independent of the traders, made no scruple of exhibiting the vices which their sons are studious to conceal. Their wants were comparatively few; the bow and arrow supplied the means of procuring large animals; from the bark of the willow they made fishing nets; the skin of the hare or the beaver sufficed them for clothing; and fire was always at their command by resort to friction. By these and the like simple means were all their necessities supplied; and there is no reason to doubt that they lived as happily as their natural disposition to indulge in war and rapine would permit. It cannot be said that the present generation is really improved by the change they have undergone in some of these respects. The trader, having in view his own sole benefit, has taught them the use of European clothing, with the addition of much superfluous finery; and their modern virtues become them about as well as these garments, and are just as consistent with their real character. In a word, those very Indians whose quiet demeanour has been so much lauded, only conceal, under this specious mask, all the vices which their fathers displayed more openly: unprovoked murder and habitual theft are committed by them whenever the opportunity offers; and their character, generally, is of a description to afford a constant source of anxiety to those who reside among them.

Such being the treacherous disposition of those Indians who, residing in the immediate vicinity of the trading posts, are in a great measure restrained by fear, and other causes co-operating, to check their evil propensities, what must he be destined to experience who wanders among the lawless tribes that are strangers to the faces of Europeans? It is the dark character of the latter that I shall here endeavour to illustrate, leaving it to my readers' judgment whether the reports that travellers have chosen to spread respecting them, are worthy of his reliance. In some of the succeeding sketches, the savage virtues are also a little shown; for what may be called virtue in the breast of a wild Indian cannot be denied them, though it may be manifested in glaring defiance of the laws of civilized society.

In 1829 I was appointed to explore the tract lying south of the Columbia, between that river and California. For five years previously I had been similarly employed to the eastward of that tract, where I had had many rencontres with the warlike tribes that cross from the east side of the Rocky Mountains to wage war with those residing on the west. War, hunting, and horse-thieving, are the sole pursuits of these reckless and most terrrible of all foragers, in the prosecution of which they have no respect for persons. The prizes they most covet are scalps and horses—it matters not whether they be snatched from trader or Indian; though, in the former case, they have been taught to purchase them more dearly than the latter. In my different meetings with them, I have been so far fortunate as to lose only three men, but it is in this quarter that drawing-room authors should travel, and I will venture to say they will return—if indeed they are so fortunate as to escape home again—with a far different impression of the character of Indians than they seem to entertain.

It was in the month of September that I bade adieu to the shores of the Columbia River, with a party composed of thirty men, well appointed, to overcome the obstacles and encounter the perils which long experience had taught me to anticipate. True, indeed, we could not boast of India-rubber pillows or boots, nor of preserved meats and soups, with many other deemed indispensable adjuncts introduced by modern travellers. However, let me confess at once the vast difference between those who travel in pursuit of amusement or science, and men like us who only encounter these hardships for vile lucre. Though we must need content ourselves with the blanket and the gun, we do, at least, possess this advantage over them, that we usually *succeed* in our arduous undertakings. On the other hand, we descend unnoticed to the grave, while honours and titles are lavished upon our rivals in enterprise!

Difficulties, many and greater than I had anticipated, began to crowd upon us; and though, by perseverance, we were enabled to surmount them, our sufferings and trials were truly great. There were times when we tasted no food, and were unable to discover water for several days together; without wood, we keenly felt the cold; wanting grass, our horses were reduced to great weakness, so that many of them died, on whose emaciated carcasses we were constrained to satisfy the intolerable cravings of our hunger, and as a last resource, to quench our thirst with their blood. Such are the privations and miseries to which Indian traders are subject in the prosecution of their precarious vocation.

After leaving the Columbia, we journeyed a month through a sterile country, before we came upon the traces of any human inhabitants, who then appeared more numerous than I had expected. On the day following their first appearance, a party consisting of ten men, who had been sent in advance as scouts, came in sight of about fifty Indians, who fled on their approach, but not soon enough to prevent the capture of two of their number. These were fully sufficient to answer all my views, which were to obtain, if possible, some information of the country before us; the amount of our knowledge at present being the course pursued, which, as indicated by the compass, was south-west. Having secured the two strangers, we treated them with all possible kindness, and by signs endeavoured to express our wishes. This is the policy adopted by all explorers of wild countries, and there surely cannot be a more humane one; although, in my opinion, which is founded on general experience, and confirmed, as will immediately appear, by the event in this particular case, it is directly opposed to the attainment of the desired end. It is something to hazard the remark, yet I will venture the opinion, that had it, on the first discovery of new countries, been resolved to treat the savages with the greatest severity, the eventual sacrifice of many lives on their own part would have been avoided, and the murderous blow averted from many an unfortunate victim, whose only offence has been the heaping of undeserved favours on wretches whose hearts were callous to the emotions of gratitude.

Having succeeded in gaining some partial information of the country in advance of us, I dismissed my informants, first presenting them with a few baubles in return. Wild as deer, they were soon out of sight, but the kind reception they had met with being, as I suppose, duly represented to their countrymen, they returned on the morrow, accompanied by a large body of men, who soon became very troublesome. Every thing about us attracted their curious attention; our horses, if possible, still more than ourselves. It was with evident reluctance that our numerous visitors left us in the evening, a few of them, indeed, hinting a wish to remain. This, I doubt not, was with the double view of observing how we secured our horses, and the precautions we took to guard against surprise, and to enable themselves to concert measures with their associates the more effectually to betray us. I gave orders to clear the camp, and for the night watch to turn out, upon which they went away.

At the dawn of day, according to my invariable custom, I had all the men aroused, the fires lighted, and the horses collected in the camp; this being the hour that Indians always fix upon for making their predatory attacks, it being then, as they say, that men sleep most soundly. In this, as in other calculations of a savage cunning, they are not far wrong. They would certainly have found it so in our case, had the precaution alluded to not been adopted; for, fatigued with the long march of the day, and wearied with anxious watching during the several divisions of the night, the long-deferred slumbers of the men were doubly sweet and sound when tired Nature could at last indulge herself. Thanks to the method we observed, every one was awake and stirring—preparing, in fact, for a start— when I perceived, in the gray dawn, a large body of Indians drawing near. When within a short distance of the camp, they hesitated to advance, as if dubious of the reception that awaited them. This had a suspicious appearance, nothing having occurred on the previous day to give rise to any doubt that it would be otherwise than friendly. We were not long left in uncertainty of their hostile intentions, for a shower of arrows was presently discharged into the camp. This was too much for our forbearance; I considered it high time to convince them that we could resent the unprovoked attack. Three of our horses were already wounded, and if we ourselves had escaped, it was probably owing to the poor beasts having sheltered us from the arrows. I therefore ordered a rifle to be discharged at them. The ball was true to its aim, and a man fell. This was sufficient as a first lesson; for on witnessing it they at once took to flight, leaving their companion dead on the field, as a mark of their evil design and its punishment. I trust they were not only duly impressed with our superiority over them, but likewise with a sense of the lenient treatment they had received, although, from past experience, I could have little hope at the time that the effect of either would be very durable.

After three days' further travelling, over a country as barren as ever Christian traversed, we came to the lands of another tribe, residing on the waters of the Rio Colorado. These Indians I strongly suspected to be the same who, the year preceding, had massacred ten men attached to the party of Mr. Smith, an American adventurer.

This ill-fated party consisted originally of thirty-five individuals, all of whom, excepting four, fell victims on this and other occasions to the blood-thirsty spirit of the natives. Though he was one of those who escaped, it would almost appear as if this enterprising American had been doomed eventually to suffer a like fate, for the following year, while on his way from St. Louis to California, for the purpose of purchasing mules and horses, he left the main party about three miles, accompanied only by two men, in quest of water. He found the object of his search, and paid for it the heavy price of his life. His protracted absence naturally exciting con-siderable alarm, though his true fate was not immediately suspected, search was made, and his body, together with those of his two companions, found stark and stiff upon the ground. The unhappy men had been murdered in cold blood, by Indians concealed in the bushes till the favourable moment arrived for the accomplishment of their ruthless purpose.

I was intimately acquainted with poor Smith, and it was from himself that I learned the particulars of his misfortunes first alluded to. As the brief story will tend to confirm my observations upon the Indian charac-ter, I will here relate it in the narrator's own words.

"After suffering severely in crossing the barren desert, I was truly well pleased," said he, "to discover a fine stream of fresh water, which proved to be the north branch of the Rio Colorado. On sounding it, I found it too deep to ford, and as grass, which my lean horses much required, appeared to be far more abundant on the opposite side, I ordered ten men of the party to get them across, which they accordingly did, by driving them into the water, and accompanying them swimming. For several days I had been unsuccessfully searching above and below our position for a ford-ing place, without discovering a vestige of any human inhabitants; but no sooner had my men landed on the opposite shore, than upwards of a hun-dred Indians rushed on them, from behind a thicket of willows, and mur-dered the whole. My horses were speedily secured and driven out of sight, and it is scarcely necessary to say that any attempt at pursuit under such circumstances had been in vain. Such was the situation in which I found myself, with property to the value of ten thousand dollars; and rather than the villains who had so deeply injured me should reap any benefit from it, I had the whole thrown into the river. We then made a raft, and crossed over, when we found the bodies of my unfortunate men so mutilated as to be scarcely recognizable. We consigned them also to the keeping of the deep, for as you well know, not even the dead are respected by the wild tribes of these parts."

The details of their now melancholy journey till their arrival at St. Gabriel, a Spanish mission in California, need not be repeated. Being unsuccessful in his errand, owing to the deficiency of his property and the mistrust with which the Spaniards viewed him as the first American who had penetrated to their settlement by land, Mr. Smith now resolved on proceeding to our depôt on the Columbia, which is known as Fort Vancouver. The Spaniards, I may remark, had subjected him to a brief confinement in prison, but being liberated through the influence of an American captain, whose ship was in the vicinity, he left St. Gabriel with the purpose I have mentioned. When within three days' journey of his new destination, being arrived on the borders of the river Umpqua, he again experienced a reverse—a more dreadful one than that already related. Here, then, I shall resume the narrative in his own words, and it will hence appear by what a slender tenure the trader holds his existence; if he escapes to return to his home, he may, indeed, thank the Almighty alone for his preservation.

It is proper to observe that myself, as well as several of our gentlemen, had on various occasions visited the village where the first treason occurred, but then we were at all times strictly on our guard. The natives, too, were sometimes in the habit of resorting to Vancouver to trade, and were well acquainted with us. They soon, however, discovered poor Smith's party to be strangers, and determined to take advantage of the misplaced confidence he seems to have reposed in their *mild* and *peaceable* disposition.

"Finding myself among Indians," he says, "whom, from their possessing many articles of European merchandize, and frequently naming you and several other gentlemen, I began to consider no longer as enemies, I relaxed my usual vigilance. Having prolonged my stay for two days, to recruit the worn-down animals I had purchased at St. Gabriel, on the third morning I directed Mr. Rogers, my assistant, to have everything in readiness, desiring the men also to clean their rifles, preparatory to start on the morrow. I then, accompanied by two men, embarked in a canoe, and proceeded in search of a suitable crossing-place, the banks opposite our encampment being too steep for the horses to surmount. On my return, after an absence of three hours, when within half a mile of the tents, I observed a number of Indians running towards us along the bank, yelling most fearfully. Immediately suspecting what had happened, we crossed over, and secreted ourselves in the bushes, the Indians discharging their guns at us without effect. Anxious to ascertain the fate of my party, I then ascended an eminence, from whence I could plainly perceive that the camp was destroyed, and not a vestige of man, horse, or mule, to be seen.

"Though conscious that the wretches would not dare to pursue us, in a country so thickly wooded, I yet considered it to be most prudent to be concealed during the day, and to travel only under cover of the night. On the second day we perceived some of the Company's servants, who conducted us safely to Vancouver."

The day preceding Mr. Smith's arrival under these circumstances, one of his party named John Black, who had escaped the massacre at the camp, had also made his way to Fort Vancouver, and preparations had at once been commenced by the superintendent of the Company's affairs, to ascertain the fate of Mr. Smith and his two men. This party was on the eve of setting out, when the arrival of the fugitives relieved us of that anxiety. From Black we elicited the particulars of the massacre in the following words: —"Soon after Mr. Smith's departure, while some of the men were cleaning their rifles, some cooking, and others trafficking with the natives, on a sudden the latter, in number exceeding two hundred, with dreadful shouts, rushed on us, before any one was prepared for defence. I," said the poor fellow, "escaped the general fate, being wounded and left for dead, but recovering, succeeded in effecting my retreat hither."

Thus fell eighteen men, far from their homes, their relations and their friends. As for the survivors, they met with every attention from us which their destitute situation demanded. Decisive measures were adopted to recover Mr. Smith's property. All the furs, with most of the horses and mules, were recovered and restored to their right owners, who subsequently made them over to the Company at a valuation rather exceeding the current price, which the agents of the Company cheerfully offered to the adventurer, in sympathy for his forlorn condition. I have only to add that his losses and misfortunes were insufficient to deter him from new enterprises. With the persevering spirit characteristic of his countrymen, he again entered the field the next year, when his career was closed as has already been related.

To return to my own situation. As I have before remarked, I strongly suspected that the Indians among whom we now found ourselves, were the same party who, the year before, had cut off part of Mr. Smith's men as first related. They appeared to be bolder than any I had yet seen; but on a narrow scrutiny, I could perceive nothing to confirm my suspicion of their identity. No tracks of horses were seen, but this was a circumstance readily accounted for by the fact that the country was too barren to admit of their being easily maintained. My men were eager to revenge the massacre upon them; but as I had no proof that these were the guilty persons, I withheld my consent to their entreaties.

That punishment, however, which I was slow to inflict on them for past deeds, of which they were doubtless guilty, they shortly drew upon themselves by present misconduct. On the day following our appearance among them, they swarmed about the camp, every man carrying, in addition to his proper arms, a long stick on his shoulder, in derision of the manner in which we carry our guns. Observing the greatness of their numbers, I took the precaution of posting an extra guard over our horses, and warned the men to hold themselves in readiness for the worst. Besides their usual fire-arms, I furnished each of our little party with a spear, giving orders not to reload after the first volley, but to charge; for I was apprehensive lest, during the interval of loading, the Indians might make a rush and overpower us; and that a speedy attack was meditated, I could no longer doubt. Our preparations completed, I admitted a few Indians into the camp, purposely that they might observe our state of defence and with the hope that it might deter them from attacking us. Unhappily for them, the desired effect was not produced, for presently one of the guard was wounded, and the alarm given that the Indians were securing our horses. This was sufficient for me. They had shed the first blood, and I was resolved that theirs should repay it; and as it was now for life or death with us, I ordered a general discharge, to be followed up by a charge with the spear. The first, however, sufficed; for on seeing the number of their fellows who in a single moment were made to lick the dust, the rest ingloriously fled, and we saw no more of them. Twenty-six remained dead on the field.

It would be inconsistent with my object to continue the narrative of the expedition, and our other travelling adventures in this region. It is not my purpose to write a book of adventure, but to illustrate, as far as my acquaintance with circumstances may enable me, and from various points of view, the character of the Indian tribes. The little I have advanced, from my own experience, may suffice to show that they do not possess the fine qualities attributed to them in recent publications, and the following sketches will make both their better and their worse characteristics still more manifest. If any one be sceptical, after all, in regard to the latter, I can only say that it would be easy to multiply instances of the most atrocious and unprovoked cruelty practised by the Indians against those engaged in the fur trade. It is enough to hint at the sad fate of Livingston, Henry, Hughes, Millar, Jones, Kennet, Smith, McKenzie, and Corrigal, chiefly officers of the service, besides nearly three hundred and fifty men, Americans and servants of the Company in nearly equal proportions, who have fallen victims within the last twenty years.

PLATE III.

The Hunter Signals the Presence of Game

CHAPTER II.

The Red Feather,

FLATHEAD CHIEF

IN the year 1823, I was appointed to the command of an expedition, destined to operate southward of the Columbia, where beaver were known to abound, which, down to that period, had never been molested by the hand of civilized man. Accordingly, during the six succeeding years, I was employed in the perilous and disagreeable duty involved in this adventure. Our party usually numbered thirty men, chiefly fur-trappers, the whole well-armed and mounted, besides each possessing a relay of thirty horses, applicable to the pack or the riding-saddle, as necessity required. Danger is an excellent disciplinarian, and since each of my followers, viewing the case through that medium, saw the necessity of strict attention to his leader's orders, I had the less difficulty in enforcing the system of precaution I have already mentioned as indispensable to the common safety; and by attention to which many tracts of country were passed over with impunity, which otherwise it would have been rash to adventure upon. The systematic order of our proceedings possessed the double advantage of enabling us to cope successfully with our foes, and to associate in confidence, when circumstances rendered it expedient to do so, with those whom we regarded as friends, at least for the time being.

On one occasion, being desirous of penetrating a tract of country more than usually infested by marauders we had to dread, I joined company with the camp of the Flathead nation, at that period proceeding on their annual visit to the buffalo-grounds. At this time, their camp consisted in all of two hundred lodges, but it was anciently much more numerous; war, in which they were continually engaged, having, within a few years, thinned off the flower of the young men, and given a preponderance to the enemy's force which sold sadly to their disadvantage. A short digression must here be permitted me by way of explaining their present position to the indulgent reader.

Residing on the headwaters of a stream tributary to the Columbia, they had been accustomed, from time immemorial, to resort to the grounds southward of their own in quest of buffalo; from the chase of which they derived their chief subsistence. In the prosecution of these annual excursions they had invariably met with much opposition and unprovoked molestation from the Blackfeet, a roving horde of real Ishmaelites, "their hand against every one, and every one's hand against them." Under ordinary circumstances, the bravery and chivalrous address of the poor Flatheads had enabled them to resent the insults of their opponents, and to repel their unprovoked attacks; but, unhappily, a few years anterior to the period of which I am writing, a fatal advantage obtained by the Blackfeet at length destroyed the balance of power, and told with murderous effect against the former. This was the acquisition of fire-arms; which implement of warfare the former obtained by traffic, through their proximity to the American frontiers, long before the more secluded Flatheads were acquainted with its use, save in its deadly effect upon the ranks of their most valued warriors. More recently, however, their intercourse with the Columbia traders had furnished the weaker party with the means of repelling the attacks of their oppressors, but not before their numbers had been reduced, through the causes alluded to, far beneath that of the rivals. Under these circumstances, they had made a compact with a small adjacent sept, called the Cootanys or Kootanais, and for mutual protection the allies proceeded to their hunting-grounds in company; their united numbers, but still more their remarkable bravery and address, now rendering them more than a match for their overbearing opponents.

Our march was conducted with much regularity; all the arrangements being overlooked by the camp chief, known among us by the appellation of "Cut Thumb." In order to assure our party as much as possible against the ordinary risks of the way, a position was allotted to us in the midst of the whole band, and which, whether in the march or when encamped, we invariably occupied. In this manner we journeyed for ten or fifteen days, occasionally meeting with a few stray buffalo, but experiencing no molestation on any hand, nor indeed seeing the vestige of an enemy. But as at sea, the calmest weather when it precedes a storm is the more to be dreaded, since the mariner is thereby lulled into treacherous security; so in these prairies, an unusual interval of peace but too frequently augurs a speedy reverse of fortune. Thus did it prove in our case. Rendered careless by the seeming absence of danger, the Indians frequently neglected the ordinary precautions necessary to secure against surprise or robbery. Their horses were left untethered and unguarded, and their proceedings generally, marked by a sense of the most careless, yet most unwarranted security.

For my own part, I maintained the usual discipline among my men, and soon had reason to congratulate myself in not having yielded to the lazy example of our Indian companions; for one morning it was found that a large number of horses had been stolen during the night, whose owners had now to lament the imprudence into which they had been tempted. Fulfilling the old proverb of "shutting the stable-door after the steed is stolen," every precautionary measure was now adopted, when no longer of any avail: scouts scoured the country on all sides; whoops, shouts, maddening yells of rage and disappointment resounded through the camp; all which gave way to soberer counsel when the result of the reconnoissance was made known by those deputed to that duty. Every concurrent circumstance pointed to their inveterate enemies, the Blackfeet Indians, as the authors of this outrage. It was also ascertained that the course of their retreat was due west, and that they were in all probability a detachment from an extensive camp whose fires were discovered in a valley some twenty miles distant.

Such was the position of affairs: council upon council was held, and my opinion consulted every hour of the day to settle some knotty point in the discussion, while I, like a skillful general, usually contrived by the wording of my decisions to avoid committing myself in the estimation of either party affected by them. To be brief, the final issue of all the arguments adduced was this; that the horses were stolen, the thieves were at hand, and that at all risks reprisals must be made. A party of young men speedily assembled, in anticipation of the adventure, but this was not definitively arranged, since one of the principal personages of the camp had remained as yet a silent but not unobservant spectator of what was passing, and without his sanction no enterprise of this nature could with propriety be undertaken. This seeming apathetic, though influential member of the band was the "Red Feather," so called from the distinctive badge he at all times wore to indicate the dignity to which by common acclamation he had been elected. His colleague the "Cut Thumb" was camp chief, and had attained the supreme dignity through his acknowledged wisdom in the affairs of every day life. The "Red Feather" was leader of the warriors, and had received his chivalrous appointment in consideration of his extraordinary prowess in the field, and the address he exhibited in all that related to martial concerns. The haughty and reserved demeanour he usually assumed was well calculated to impress his companions with a lofty opinion of his character; while his suavity of manner when addressed, tended to secure for him their regard and esteem. Bold and fearless, he was at the same time prudent and skillful beyond any Indian who roved the prairies: his renown was spread far and wide; and among all the Flathead warriors there was not one whose name resounded so frequently in the Blackfeet camp, when the lamentations of the bereaved told of valued racers disappeared, or the wail of widows gave signal of deeds of death. Tall, well-shaped, and muscular, his person exhibited every characteristic of strength and activity; while his features were marked by well-cut, expressive outlines, which would have distinguished him to the most casual observer as a man of character and ability. Such in outward seeming was the "Red Feather," towards whom at this critical period, every eye was turned in expectation of counsel.

When at length his long-deferrred judgment was delivered, the hasty preparations that had been undertaken on the spur of the moment were rendered void, since all immediate retaliation was discountenanced by the old warrior. "Peace for a while," said he; "let us not be hasty: the Blackfeet are even now on their guard against our enterprises, and would frustrate them. Let us send the pipe of peace towards them, and meet them as friends: time rolls on, and we shall yet be quits with them before the grass is withered on the prairie."

The advice was acted upon: after an interchange of messages, a grand meeting was agreed to, and the spot of the conference fixed. It was a level part of the plain, bordering on a small stream that meandered lazily through the boundless expanse of the surrounding prairies. A few willows skirted the brook in some favoured spots, but in general the arid banks produced but the coarse prairie grass, diversified in certain low bottoms, where the moisture of the brook soaked through the soil, by patches of wild vetch, and rank thickets of hemlock—a baneful weed which thrives wondrously in these sequestered regions.

Repairing hither at the appointed time, we found the Blackfeet already posted to receive us; and after a due allowance of ceremonial preparations, we proceeded to the business of the day, with all the consequence and sincerity of practised diplomatists. At the head of the Flathead party, by virtue of his dignity of peace-chief, rode our notable leader the "Cut Thumb," attended by the pipe-bearer and a varlet of no small importance in his own esteem, who carried the bag of medicine. The "Red Feather" and myself followed close behind, representing the native prowess and allied strength of the clan; while the rear was brought up by a gallant cavalcade of warriors, who fretted their steeds with knee and bridle, making them caracole as they rode along, in order to show off their skill in the *menage*. The cavaliers of the opposite party were not a whit inferior to them in these knightly accomplishments, and bestrode their ill-gotten animals with an air of the most consummate self-possession.

To the imposing display of these first approaches to each other, succeeded the pipe of peace, and other affectations of friendship; all which being happily ended, the assembly was repeatedly harangued by the orators on both sides, who, if they wanted the euphonical polish of a Cicero, might have vied with Demosthenes in the energetic vigour of their language. On the part of the Flatheads, a recapitulation of grievances from time immemorial opened the discussion: this was met by an argument having much the same tendency, and yet more point, in behalf of the opposite faction. "You complain," said they, "that we have stolen your horses! While you are speaking the blood of our young men whom you have slain is yet warm; their scalps are not dry that you took from us. You say that in days past, before your white fathers gave you guns, we killed many of you! Has not your revenge been complete? Only last year twenty of our warriors were cut off as with fire; three of their scalps even now decorate the 'Red Feather,' who stands before us. You, 'Cut Thumb,' you—you who now accuse us of injuring the Flatheads—with your spells and incantations have cast sickness into our camp: our children gasp for breath, our very horses are less fleet than was their wont, solely owing to your strong medicines, and the virulence of your hatred towards us. As for the horses you have lost, the *Shoshonies* must have taken them; not one has entered our camp: our young men are low spirited and are become as women; how then could they have done so bold an action?" In this strain of mutual recrimination and defence the parley was carried on to the end; both parties pretending to believe implicitly the expressions of good will and peaceful intentions lavishly poured forth, yet each inwardly chuckling at the other's credulity. A hollow peace was eventually patched up by these punic diplomatists, and the two camps separating, went afterwards each on its way, in the direction where they expected to find buffalo.

Three days afterwards the "Red Feather" came to my tent. "Today I go for horses," said he: "the Blackfeet are unsuspicious; my young men have seen their camp; their horses are unwatched. The Black," added he, alluding to one which had attracted my attention from the symmetry of its shape—"the Black must be mine at all risks." Attended by two of his followers, he went off the same night, not as usual on horseback, but on foot, each of the party carrying a small supply of dried meat, and a tough *lasso* that sufficiently declared the nature of their mission.

Meanwhile we had fallen upon buffalo. Immense herds of these uncouth beasts ranged over the prairie, which was intersected in every direction by the deeply-worn paths of their periodical migrations. The grand business of the year now commenced in good earnest: the hunters prepared their trained racers for the duties of the chase; everything was put in readiness; but no man ventured to leave the precincts of the camp. At length the chief, having ascertained that all the preparations were complete, gave the welcome signal—proclaiming, in a loud voice, that all were now at liberty to depart, and adding such recommendations as seemed necessary for maintaining order among the multitude. Joy beamed from every face; the very horses seemed alive to the excitement of the occasion; and as they drew near the buffalo, could with difficulty be restrained. The whole cavalcade, consisting of some three hundred horsemen, were shortly engaged indiscriminately in the herd.

At first the poor victims stood eyeing their approaching enemies; then, as if mistrusting the nature of their intentions, they began to move slowly off in a body; their sullen walk soon changing to an awkward gallop, and as their rear and flanks became more and more pressed by their pursuers, ending in a general rout. Now was the crisis of the chase, and the hunter's opportunity, when he showed his skill, not to mention his good taste, by selecting the fattest animals as they scuttled over the plain. Shot after shot resounded in every direction; while the scarcely less fatal arrow did its share in the general work of destruction, only more silently. The horses, trained to the task, seemed as if intuitively acquainted with what was required of them; keeping even pace with the selected animal, and preserving, at all times, a distance of several paces from its side; watching pointedly its every motion, and lightly springing away whenever it would gore them, as if anticipating its intentions even before they were put in practice.

Several hundred animals lay scattered in every direction around us. In the distance the retreating herds were rushing wildly over the plain, sometimes enveloped in dust, then emerging from the cloud and becoming again visible as the flickering wind shifted athwart, or in the line of their course. Here and there a scattered horseman, more eager or better mounted than the rest, still pursued the flying bands; while a dropping shot, from time to time, sounded the knell of another victim. The hunters began to congregate, and the division of the prey alone was wanting to finish the day's proceedings. Suddenly a cloud of dust appeared on the horizon, in the direction of our preceding day's march. All eyes were strained to discover the cause. There were no buffalo in that quarter to account for the commotion; but all conjecture was soon put at rest: the peculiar cry with which the Indian jockeys urge on a band of horses, maddening them by some strange sympathy beyond conception, was heard from time to time, repeated with growing distinctness as the excited horses approached; a yell of welcome broke forth, when at length a numerous band became discoverable, driven by three mounted Indians, who were soon recognized as the "Red Feather" and his two daring associates. As they drew near it might be seen that the horses were well-nigh exhausted; the foam, trickling down their quivering flanks, mingled with the accumulated dust, and completely disguised their exterior features. Anon they would slacken their pace, and seek momentary relief by snatching languidly at the tufts of grass around them; but the shrill and piercing whoop, whose strangely discordant modulation it were vain to endeavour to express, or even to imitate, would again set them off with redoubled energy, its strange unearthly sound seeming to act like enchantment upon the muscular frames of the animals, through its influence over the inward faculties. What the cause of this peculiar sympathy between man and beast may be, or what connection between the cry in question and the extraordinary effect produced by it, is not in my power to determine; but the fact is too commonly known, and too well authenticated to admit of doubt. In this instance I was deeply struck by the singular infatuation of the poor jaded brutes. Wearied to exhaustion, they yet seemed to rise superior to all bodily weakness, as soon as they heard the cry of their persecutors in the rear. On they rushed; death, destruction might be before them; fire, or a precipice, might intercept their path; but it seemed as if no obstacle could for a moment check their progress while under this strange spell.

Arriving at the camp, the "Red Feather" and his two associates dismounted at a bound, slipped the cords in an instant out of their horses' mouths, and turning them loose, uttered a loud whew of complacency, finishing with a hearty laugh at the success of their exploit. After their hunger had been appeased with a supply of boiled meat proportionate to their long fast, served to them in the principal lodge, the endless pipe was lighted, and they recounted the hazards they had undergone; to which, though one would have supposed some of the incidents not to be over agreeable, they invariably gave a ludicrous or jocund turn. Their delighted audience listened with infinite relish to the story of this adventure; the braves relating how they had overheard the luckless Blackfeet boasting in their camp, and chuckling over their fancied security. "But," said the "Red Feather," in conclusion, and in a tone of disappointment, "the Black was left behind after all. I visited in one night almost every tent in the camp; for he was not loose with the band. I crept on my belly among the horses' feet, and sought and sought to no purpose. At length I found him. He was tied, but not tethered with a picket: his master held the cord as he slept; the day was breaking, or I would have cut it." Then, warming again with the remembrance of his successful foray, the chivalrous rogue declared that he would yet bestride the gallant black steed.

A month had elapsed since the events I have narrated. Our camp had for a time been stationary in a position not far from the scene of the "Red Feather's" exploit. My own movements, however, had not been restrained by the inactivity of my Indian allies. Accompanied by my party, whom I considered strong enough to resist any open attack, and sufficiently disciplined to run little danger of being reduced or pillaged by stratagem, I had made a distant excursion in quest of beaver; roving about among the small brooks which intersect the country and communicate with the larger streams by which the waters are carried towards the south branch (Lewis and Clarke's), and thence to the Columbia. Success had attended our endeavours in a signal degree; and desirous of acquiring additional information concerning the neighbourhood, before finally separating from the native camp, and shaping my course southward, I was at present allowing a few days' repose to our wearied horses. As for the Indians, they were mostly employed in the grave operations of the preserved meat and leather business, for which the capital in hand had been found by the poor buffalo. Scaffolds surrounded the camp in all directions, garnished with jerked meat, undergoing the process of desiccation; partly effected by the sun's rays, and partly by the smouldering fires maintained beneath. Elsewhere might be seen large frames fashioned of poles tied together, upon which the skins of the animals who had furnished these supplies for many future banquets and merrymakings, were spread to dry, either in their natural state, intended for coverings, or with the hair detached, in preparation for cutting into cords, or for other use useful purposes. Everywhere, I may here remark, only women were visible in active employment; for upon them the whole duty of the camp developed, even to the "hewing of wood and drawing of water;" their lordly masters thinking themselves quit of all obligation by the slaughter of the animals of the chase and the defence of their camp against the invasion of their hereditary enemies the Blackfeet. At high noon, the "lords of the creation" might be observed lazily stretched out, sunning themselves upon their extended buffalo robes; or idly visiting the precincts of the camp in quest of some favourite charger. Here and there a young stripling exercised a yearling colt to the cord, or was engaged in breaking-in some refractory member of his parent's teams to the bridle or the burthen—perhaps indulging himself with a gallop, barebacked, among the lodges, exhibiting the paces of his steed with the intention of attracting the gaze of some tawny-visaged damsel. Within the lodges, the men were either napping lazily as in the sunnier spots outside, or still worse, wiling away the time with the excitement of gambling.

This vicious propensity is the bane of savage life; as it often proves of more civilized communities. Horses, guns, blankets, whatever the poor Indian can call his own, is ruthlessly sacrificed to this Moloch of human weakness.

The hour was noon, the scene such as I have described. A listless enervation pervaded the camp, occasioned by the extreme heat; for it was now midsummer. Groups of children were amusing themselves, as happier children are wont to do, shaded under the mimic lodges they had erected;

their noisy prattling alone disturbing the general stillness. I had been some days expecting the arrival of the "Red Feather," who was again off in quest of the coveted Black so often mentioned. It was important to my views that I should see the chief, since his knowledge of a particular section of the country qualified him in an eminent degree to advise me on some points necessary to the success of the expedition. My impatience increased daily, and I was anxiously looking out for his arrival, when, at the time mentioned, a cry was raised which betokened an approaching party.

The whole camp was speedily on the outlook to discover the name and quality of their visitors. At first, only a cloud of dust was visible, but presently a single horseman, approaching at a gallop, gave rise to additional conjecture. When he drew near, the son-in-law of "Red Feather" was recognized; but he uttered no cry: his horse was wearied to the last extremity, scarcely could its tottering legs sustain the weight of the body as it galloped painfully towards us. Portentous tidings were doubtless on the eve of reaching us; not a voice was lifted to inquire their tenor, as if everyone intuitively anticipated evil. In a few moments, the weary beast came panting up to the lodges, and the tidings of his rider were delivered in a few sad words; leaping hastily to the ground, he only said:—"'Red Feather' is no more, he is gone the way of his fathers!" Then arose the cry of the fatherless and the widow; the wail of the companion and the friend. The silence that had before prevailed was now contrasted by the heart-rending expressions of mourning uttered on all sides; and the camp, lately so listless and peaceable, resounded with one general wail of grief and lamentation.

The death of the noble chief of the Flathead warriors, according to the account of his surviving companion, was most tragical. The adventurers had reached the precincts of the Blackfeet camp unobserved, and after much skilful manœuvering had succeeded in securing the envied Black, together with the horse on which the witness had reached his own camp, as they were feeding in open day in a meadow close by the lodges. They had scarcely time to mount their prizes when they were discovered. Giving rein to their steeds they uttered a shout of defiance, and struck in the direction of home, pursued after a short interval by a numerous party of the enemy. But they were safe from pursuit. They had, as they knew, secured the two fleetest runners of the band, and set at nought all the endeavours of their pursuers to overtake them. Prompted by the dictates of their fury, the latter resorted to a common expedient to wreak their vengeance.

The wind, which had till now been scarcely perceptible, began to blow freshly from the river. The "Red Feather," whose horse showed not the least symptom of distress, had reined him up and stopped for some minutes as if in defiance of the enemy. Suddenly the pursuing party stopped, and in a moment a bright blaze gave warning to the "Red Feather" that no time was to be lost; they had set fire to the plain. Driven by the fierce wind, the flame advanced with surprising speed: a broad strip of marly soil destitute of all vegetation lay before them, beyond which the fire could not pass. To reach this was their only chance of safety. The distance was easily accomplished by the narrator, since he was close to the margin when the flames arose; but the "Red Feather" was less fortunate; his act of defiance cost him his life. When in safety himself the Indian turned to ascertain the progress of his father-in-law. He was within a quarter of a mile of the desired haven. The Black strove gallantly to reach it, but all his efforts were useless; the raging element, fed with the dry grass, advanced with the speed of an eagle. A short few moments and all was over. The "Red Feather" lay a blackened corpse among the smoking ashes, his gallant steed beside him! Such was the melancholy end of the boldest warrior of the Flathead tribe, whose renown yet lives among the wild races to whom his name was in days of yore familiar.

Shortly after this melancholy event I separated from the brave and hospitable tribe that it had plunged into mourning; and of whom it is but due to remark, that of all the tribes on the west side of the Rocky Mountains they stand pre-eminently alone, in not having shed the blood of a white man. My journey to the Columbia was effected in six weeks—not, however, without undergoing considerable anxiety and privation; all which was soon forgotten in the hearty welcome I received from my worthy friend B——, who shortly before had been appointed to that station.

CHAPTER III.

The Burial of the Dead and the Living

I ONCE witnessed a strange occurrence, which, after repeated inquiries, I find to be an isolated instance of what may excite perhaps no little surprise—the voluntary interment of a living Indian. Four other gentlemen were present at this tragedy, for such it may truly be called, and should this narrative ever meet their eyes they will readily bear testimony to its correctness. The circumstances gave occasion to many remarks at the time, more especially among ourselves, for we could with difficulty conceive a human being possessing so much perverted resolution as to sacrifice himself in a manner so dreadful: but the facts were obvious, and all surmises vanished before them.

Suicides, indeed, are of such constant occurrence among civilized nations, as to excite little comment, and the circumstances of the crime are often of almost incredible horror. It is well known that they are less frequent among savage tribes; and if they are more common among some of these unfortunate people than others, it will generally be found that they are committed under some momentary impulse of desperate excitement. Instances of calm, resolute self-destruction, such as that I am about to relate, are certainly of rare occurrence. It is worthy of remark, also, that the proportion of suicides among the females, far exceeds that of the males, the causes for which I do not pretend to assign, though they may reasonably be sought in the cruel usage to which they are subject.

It was in the autumn of 1825, two days after my arrival at Wallawalla, near the confluence of the north and south branches of the Columbia, after an absence of eleven months. I was enjoying the long disused luxury of a glass of wine, in company with Mr. D—— and his companions, when a young Indian entered, and requested the presence of the former gentleman at his tent. The visit was rather a long one, and on his return, Mr. D—— informed us that the "Eagle," a chief of this place, had lost a son, who had just breathed his last. This was the second of his children who had died within a few months, and the bereaved father appeared to be in a very desponding state in consequence. His wife, however, was still alive, and there likewise remained two married daughters to comfort his declining days. Riches, too, were his, if these could have afforded him any consolation; for, possessing more than a hundred horses, he ranked among the opulent of the tribe. Unhappily, notwithstanding all that yet remained to him, life had lost its charm. All his hopes and all his desires had been centered in his departed sons — his only stay in the decline of life — for whose sakes any sacrifice would have been endured, and for whose premature fate no mourning in his eyes seemed sufficient.

The interment of the corpse was appointed to take place on the following day; but the deceased not being one of our number, no impression was made on us by the announcement. Far otherwise had it been one of our own companions in adventure; for the death of a friend in these savage wilds has generally a deep and lasting effect on his fellow-sojourners; and although it be the common lot of humanity, yet the idea of dying in this country, without, perhaps, one loved heart to soothe the dying moments, and without the participation in that holy rite which reassures us of mercy hereafter, is indeed a melancholy prospect.

Such were the circumstances, under which one of those assembled on this occasion, poor D——, some years afterwards yielded up his breath. He was a good-hearted, generous fellow, and much respected by all who knew him. Our school days had been passed together, and the friendship then contracted, increased instead of diminishing with increasing years. Poor fellow! Little did he or I then anticipate so early a termination to his earthly career, which he fulfilled in a manner alike honourable to his head and his heart.

D—— was invited to attend the burial; and being the commandant of the establishment, could not with propriety refuse showing this mark of respect to the family of the chief. The invitation was likewise extended to the other gentlemen and myself, for whom the same inducement did not exist, so that, in short, we felt disposed to decline. Yielding to the persuasion of D——, however, we accompanied him, and, as the event turned out, I was not sorry we did so. The scene we witnessed was unparalleled in my experience, and though horrifying in the extreme, it was yet, from its very strangeness, of absorbing interest.

The grave was dug on a small eminence, some furlongs distant from the fort. On reaching the spot we found an immense concourse of natives assembled, among whom the father and family of the deceased were conspicuous. The former stood on the brink of the grave, in a desponding mood; and though he permitted no outward symptom of grief to appear, it was yet evident to all that a mighty and continued effort alone kept it in restraint. He appeared to be about fifty years of age, and his form and features, though stern and swarthy, offered a model of manly beauty. The mother and her daughters were loud in their expressions of grief; but that of the father, from its very calmness, was the more terrible, and I could not but sympathize with feelings so obviously acute.

The weeping and wailing of the assembled friends were the only sounds to be heard, and for a long while the business for which they were assembled was suspended, as if no one was willing to impose the last trial of their hearts upon the bereaved parents. At length the father gave a stern order that the body should be deposited in the grave; a mandate which was reluctantly obeyed by her who had equal cause to mourn their great loss. The old man then commanded silence, and in a resolute tone of voice began to address the assembled multitude. Having called attention to the different events of his life, as connected with the rank he occupied, he proceeded to remind them—always addressing himself to Mr. D——, —of the domestic afflictions he had endured, concluding with the recent death of his eldest and most beloved son, whose corpse was now before us. "And now," said he, "the string of my bow is broken, the last hope of my declining days has forsaken me. Seek not to dissuade me from the resolution I have adopted, for I am resolved upon following him, and all you can urge will be in vain; life has no longer any charm for me. I was once a hunter, but am now no longer so; I was once the proud father of two noble sons; but, alas! where are they? I was once a warrior, but am no longer so. Wherefore shall I continue to cumber this earth with my useless presence?"

The silence that now prevailed was so deep that not even a breath was audible. The old man folded his blanket around him, cast one farewell look on the fair fields and the broad-rolling river in the vicinity; and then, to the surprise of all present, descended composedly into the pit, and laid himself upon the corpse of his departed son. "Throw in the earth, fill up the grave, cover up my last earthly residence," exclaimed he. "Nay, do not hesitate, for I am resolved to die." Screams of agony arose from his afflicted wife and daughters; vehement expostulations were resorted to by all around; but the old chief remained firm. Not the tenderest entreaties of those who were dearest to him among the living—not the eager representations of his friends, backed by the usually influential voice of D——, could, for an instant, shake the resolve of the self-devoted victim. "I will die!" said he; "seek no longer to prevent it; I repeat it, I will die!"

When it was found that all expostulations and entreaties were in vain, the friends held a clamorous council among themselves, which resulted in a decision to obey the will of the chief. When he saw that his wish would be complied with, he again spoke, and gave directions for the disposal of his property: his horses were ordered to be divided among his relations, ten of the finest being first given to Mr. D——, who was looked upon by the Indians as an adopted father.

Meanwhile I had advanced to the brink of the grave, in order to observe narrowly the countenance of the old man. I could perceive no symptoms of weakness. The same stern calmness which was at first perceptible, still continued to characterize it, and as the clods of earth began to shower down upon him, still not a muscle relaxed. In the midst of the most fearful howlings and lamentations were the horrid obsequies performed; the clay and the sand being filled in, the green sod was at length carefully arranged over the small spot which marked the last resting-place of the *living and the dead.*

Agreeably to the last request of the "Eagle," Mr. D—— caused a flag to be placed over his grave, the tattered remnants of which still fluttered in the breeze when I last visited the spot; serving to indicate to the passer-by the scene of the horrid though voluntary sacrifice I have related.

CHAPTER IV.

An Indian Festival

SIX years ago, being the spring of 1832, I was stationed on the north-west coast of America, at the recently-formed settlement of Fort Simpson, at the mouth of the Nass River. This establishment was the only one as yet maintained there, and its erection was so recent, that our knowledge of the savage tribes in the midst of whom we were settled, was very scanty. At this particular season, the natives from all quarters are in the habit of assembling on the shores of the Nass, for the purpose of obtaining a supply of small fish, of delicate flavour, termed *Olichon*, which resort to this stream in innumerable shoals to spawn, and afford active employment during the brief season they remain, to the native fishermen.

Although at all times most guarded to avoid any surprise from our rude neighbours, the overpowering numbers thus congregated from all quarters in our immediate vicinity, gave an additional spur to our vigilance; and the need of watchfulness will be apparent, when I add that the whole garrison, including myself and the other officers, did not exceed twenty men. With this insignificant force it became us to exercise unremitted attention, and certainly every one gave himself to the harassing task with a zeal which the occasion fully demanded.

One morning in April, I observed, and remarked to one of the gentle-men, that the natives were assembling in unusual force immediately in front of the gates, and we both agreed that it had a suspicious appearance.

PLATE IV.
The Chief Orders a Hunt

We remained in suspense for some minutes, when one of the principal chiefs came to our little fortress, demanding admission, as he had something of importance to impart to me. The formal manner in which this request was made increased instead of diminishing my anxious curiosity. He was ushered into my room of state, a chamber set apart expressly for the reception of the great men of the land. I observed that he took the precaution of closing the doors, and though I was under no apprehension of present danger to myself, the stranger being completely in my power, I nevertheless, and very naturally, felt some misgivings as to the purpose of a morning call attended with so much formality.

Being seated, the chief remained some time in silence, and then, as if moved by the spirit, commenced as follows: —"Great Chief of the Whites, you are too vigilant not to have observed an unusual concourse of my young men in front of your fort; they are there by my orders, and without evil design. It is my intention to give a great feast. We are come here to make preparations for it, and I require your assistance."

It is scarcely necessary to say that such a solution of the mystery was very much to my satisfaction, and that I cheerfully complied with the request of the grand steward of the forthcoming banquet. Canoes continued going and coming every day and hour, all freighted with cargoes of dingy savages. For ten mortal days, not a moment of tranquillity was experienced; the concourse of Indians at last assembled on the ground exceeding, on the most moderate calculation, 1,500 souls. The preparations for the feast were of course on a proportionately grand scale—at least as far as labour and expense were concerned. A lot of deals, recently received, amounting to about a thousand, were put in requisition, and employed by the natives to erect a temporary shed for the accommodation of the guests; while other articles necessary to their operations were borrowed, as wanted, from us.

Our vigilance, it may be imagined, did not abate under these circumstances, of the sincerity of which we had no guarantee. We had property in our warehouse to a large amount, offering a great temptation to their cupidity, and, indeed, other considerations apart, had no inclination to put their forbearance to the test, or to submit ourselves to their tender mercies. The two gentlemen who were with me merited, however, all my confidence, and this relieved my mind of a great load of anxiety. Truly may it be said, that Indian traders experience severe trials in the course of their duty; not to mention the privations which they cheerfully undergo. Alas! that many who look forward for the reward of tranquillity and repose at last do so, too often in vain, frequently cursing the day they ever left their homes to pass their lives among Indians.

At length, all the great preliminaries being finished, the hour was at hand when the affair was to "come off." On the eleventh day, shortly after sunrise, two Indians carrying a long pole, at the end of which were suspended feathers of the bald-headed eagle, came to the fort gates, and with a loud voice desired admittance to the white chief. Their request being granted, they advanced into the hall, and after duly performing their obeisance, touched with their wands of office myself and the two gentlemen who were present with me.

This grand ceremony, we were given to understand, was to be construed into an invitation to attend the entertainment of the day, to commence about noon. We now held a consultation concerning the propriety of accepting an invitation of this nature; after duly weighing the arguments for and against such a show of complaisance, I decided on doing so, and that one of the gentlemen, the surgeon, should likewise attend; thus setting at nought the vague rumours of evil intended against us, which we could not avoid hearing. We first made every arrangement with the gentleman who remained at home, respecting the measures he should adopt in the event of treachery, and then, accompanied by six men and our body guard, proceeded to the house of feasting, which, if I might conjecture future events by the lugubrious visages of the men, was likely to prove to some of us a house of mourning. The building was erected within a hundred yards of the fort, and to suggest the idea that we were prepared to revenge any treacherous measures, two field-pieces were exposed in a commanding situation in the block-houses.

On our arrival at the entrance of the banqueting hall, which the Indians had extemporized with considerable skill, we found the crowd so great that ingress was for a moment impossible. A frightful howling and shouting, however, soon drew attention to our presence, and six stout fellows, whose office of masters of the ceremonies seemed blended with that of special constables to preserve the public peace on this occasion, laid about them with such right good-will and effect that a wide passage was opened for us, and the jackall-like howls of the expectant revellers partially quelled as they retired on either side. In this state we entered the building, which we found to be of very ample dimensions, provided also, at one end, with an elevated stage, before which a parti-coloured curtain was suspended. The whole of the remaining area was occupied by rows of seats arranged as in the pit of a theatre, the *tout ensemble*, indeed, forcibly reminding me of the plan of arrangement adopted in places of that description, in more polished situations than a scarcely known spot of the north-west coast of this continent. As the honoured guests of the chief, we were accommodated with a couple of chairs within a short distance of the stage, and during the brief interval occurring before the attention was otherwise demanded, had a favourable opportunity of computing the number of Indians present, which could not have been less than eight hundred, exclusive of women, who were seated apart, and of a crowd of slaves of both sexes, who eagerly thronged the entrance with the hope of witnessing the grand doings about to proceed within-doors.

A stop was soon put to my speculations on this point, by the elevation of the curtain which immediately followed a signal proceeding from behind it. On the stage, boldly erect, stood the lord of the banquet, recognizable by his lofty stature and the stately proportions which imparted a peculiar grace and dignity to his bearing. On his face he wore a grotesque mask of wood. More interesting still, his head was surmounted by an emblematical figure, representing the sun, rendered luminous by some simple contrivance in the interior. As all eyes were turned upon him, the stage was so arranged that he gradually disappeared beneath it, bearing with him the source of light by which our artificial little world was illuminated, and leaving us in total darkness; a state of affairs which, knowing the savagely treacherous characters with whom we were associated, was by no means agreeable to us white men. The matter was so contrived, however, that daylight presently began to appear again, until, by slow degrees, our Indian Phœbus, bearing the bright orb of day, whose temporary absence we had deplored, stood erect before us in all the meridian splendour of his first appearance.

Three times was this alternate setting and rising of the sun repeated, each repetition eliciting rounds of rapturous applause, expressed by shouts, screams, howlings, and gesticulations, most indescribably appalling, and such as might cause a momentary shudder to the stoutest heart. To do our entertainer justice, his performance, simple as it was, was most creditably carried through, and spoke much in favour of the native talent of its orig-inator. The deception by which the gradual appearance and disappearance of the light was imitated, was indeed most complete, and productive of much satisfaction to us all. Then came the second act of this dramatic rep-resentation, consisting in a grand dance performed in the true North-west Coast style, by forty young women, each rejoicing in a choice article of feminine trinketry inserted, *secundum artem*, in the lower lip. Their mo-tions, as my friend the surgeon remarked — for I myself am no judge of these affairs — were in perfect unison with the music of a chorus sung by the dancers themselves; and although they had not enjoyed the advan-tages of instruction under Italian masters of the art, they at least contorted their limbs to as good purpose as is usual in exhibitions of a like nature.

The dancing having continued for half an hour, the exhibition ceased, but there was yet no sign of the promised feast, beyond the strong odour of putrid oil which pervaded the place, and which indicated the existence of something in the shape of eatables in the vicinity. The delay was pres-ently explained when the chief entered the arena of the hall, followed by slaves bearing presents. He laid at my feet five beautiful sea-otter skins, & a quantity of beaver, while a proportionable quantity fell to the share of my companion. Furs, war-dresses, slaves, and other property, were then dis-tributed in adequate portions among the assembled chiefs. The slaves, poor unfortunates! though thus transferred to strangers, viewed the change with a seeming indifference, well knowing that, here or elsewhere, slavery was their inevitable lot, and that it was scarcely possible to change for the worse. Pity that the Slavery Emancipation Act does not extend its influence to these remote shores, where the labours and sufferings of these unhappy wretches whose condition it might ameliorate, cease only with death.

Immense piles of meat and north-west delicacies of all descriptions now appeared, and judging from the concourse of guests, I considered they were sufficient to consume the whole, without assistance on my part. Perhaps I may here acknowledge, without much danger of wounding the sensibility of my kind entertainers, that I felt little desire to partake of their good cheer, having strong and not unreasonable misgivings that human flesh might compose an undistinguishable portion; it being known, in fact, that slaves are frequently sacrificed as a *bonne bouche* to grace the repast. Having intimated our desire to the chief, the word was instantly given to make way for our departure. The officious masters of the ceremonies, as prompt in obedience as command, instantly obeyed the mandate, and in a few moments we emerged into the open air, honoured as we went by the same unearthly shouts that had greeted our arrival. This mode of salutation, until we grew accustomed to it, caused us some surprise: all over the interior it is usual for the natives to remain, on the arrival of strangers, more than usually quiet, so that conversation, or remarks of any kind, seldom commence till the introductory pipe of ceremony has made the tour of those assembled.

As for our friendly convives, whose hospitality we may have failed to appreciate, they passed a sleepless, though doubtless an agreeable night, & daylight the next morning found them still revelling in the excess of their enjoyment. A few hours more, and the remembrance of all this jollity was all that remained to rejoice their lodges in the wilderness. The slaves of the entertainers speedily demolished their grand banqueting-hall; replaced the deals as they found them; and, to their honour be it said, restored all borrowed articles. Best of all, they incontinently took their own departure, leaving us once more in that state of comparative ease and tranquillity which their grand revel had so long and so disagreeably interrupted.

CHAPTER V.

A Tale of Western Caledonia

TEN or twelve years are now elapsed since I was stationed at Fort Killmaurs, in the Babine country, on the sea~ ~rd frontier of Western Caledonia. Since then I have been a wanderer far and near, my perverse fate never permitting me to sojourn long in the same spot; but driving me about without cessation, like a ball in a tennis-court. While in the heyday of youth, this vagrant kind of life was not without its charms to one of my unsettled disposition: with advancing years, however, soberer tastes, and less adventurous desires have crept over me, until I could heartily wish for a life of greater tranquillity. The potentates who rule my destiny seem, however, otherwise inclined, and I now discover, to my overpowering chagrin and discomfort, that what I began willingly, and regarded as amusement, I must continue in earnest and against the grain, like physic administered to one who might wish it "to the dogs"—"*le flux, m'amena le reflux m'amene.*" When, oh, when, will this life of involuntary peregrination cease?

But a truce to useless plaints, and let me ask you, the happy reader of my sometimes unhappy narrations, if you have ever been in Western Caledonia? If you have not, I must tell you that Fort Killmaurs, my old charge, is situated on the borders of a superb lake, called by the natives "Nata," by ourselves denominated "Babine." Wherefore this difference of name? and what the origin of the latter? you may perhaps ask. Know, then, that the inhabitants of the vicinity, like those of the neighbouring sea-coast, have a strange custom of inserting pieces of wood, or ivory, in the shape of small platters, concave on both sides, into perforations made in the nether lips of the fairer portion of the community. Jean Baptiste, a Canadian, having a nice eye for analogy of form, and detecting the likeness of this self-imposed deformity to the *babine*, or lip of a cow, or a horse, saw no better way of perpetuating his discovery than its immediate application as the distinguishing name of the tribe. This delicate appellation has since taken a place in the nomenclature of the country, of which it would be now difficult to deprive it; notwithstanding the frequent inconvenience which is allowed on all hands to result from the arbitrary mode of naming places, without reference to the aboriginal nomenclature, by which alone they ought to be distinguished.

Fort Killmaurs, at the date of my present story, had been established about a year only. It had been my lot to superintend the cutting of the first stick at its commencement, and to witness the hoisting of the British flag. It is scarcely credible how expeditiously *forts* are "knocked up," and what is meant by their *completion*, in this country. After this epoch, to which I had for some time, and most anxiously looked forward, I began to feel more at ease, as, happen what might, we had now the means of ensuring our safety in the event of any sudden rupture with the swarthy savages who surrounded us. The sense of security, and the leisure which a year of anxiety at length left me, was favourable to the consideration of plans for acquiring a more intimate knowledge of the surrounding country. Several projects presented themselves to my mind, all smacking more or less of adventure, until it became utterly impossible to remain quietly ensconced in my chimney-corner. I at length determined, as a *premier pas*, on paying a visit to the village of Hotset, which, the natives informed me, was situated at some days' march distance, on the borders of a large stream, of which that issuing from the Nata Lake was a tributary. Following up this resolve, I speedily put affairs in train for its due prosecution: in the first place, making such dispositions as I deemed necessary for the safety of the post during my absence, and consigning the charge to my junior in command. I then selected such of the servants as I wished to accompany me, and set forward on my voyage of discovery.

There is something animating in the very name of an expedition to explore new countries, and how much more in the actual prosecution of one! Who, while only perusing the history of another's wanderings, has not experienced a feeling, however slight, of envy, as each wayside adventure is reproduced with life-like distinctness in the magic mirror of his imagination? Who in his reveries upon the romance of travel has not felt his heart bound with the zest of discovery, seasoned with the humour of a Bruce or a Le Vaillant; or who but has sympathized with the hopes and the fears, & the daily disappointments of some adventurous Park, or equally adventurous Clapperton? Alas, for us poor north-westers! we can only envy the fame of these renowned names. But, as I have said, there is something which tends to exalt the mind in the prospect of exploring regions till now trodden only by the footsteps of the savage; something which gives a higher tone to all our feelings, calling every talent of observation into play, and provoking curiosity which one is willing to strain every nerve to gratify. *Mais, revenons a nos moutons*. On leaving Fort Killmaurs, our route lay towards the end of the lake. A large canoe, manned by ten select men, skimmed over the waters in regatta style; the adjacent shores echoing the songs of the rowers, as they bent to the oars, and one after another caught up the exhilarating chorus. The pleasure of riding over the waters, the pure air, the panorama of the unknown shores, and the cheerful songs of my companions, all contributed to the balmy feeling of gladness which came over me, as I mused on the adventures which lay before us. I was by no means confident of a welcome reception when we should arrive at our destination, and was moreover well aware that it was the rendezvous of all the blackguards and all the gamblers of the surrounding villages. I had, however, taken every precaution to ensure our safety as far as the arming of the party went; and it now only remained, by a judicious line of conduct, to avoid all occasion of rupture with the natives of Hotset, to whom the faces and manners of Europeans were as yet unknown.

A few hours served to take us to Nasschick, a village occupied by some of the Lake Indians. This village, or rather hamlet, is situated at the extremity of the Nata, at a point where the opposite shores, gradually converging for some distance, approach each other so nearly as to indicate, at the first glance, the commencement of the stream by which the waters of the lake are discharged.

We were received here with great demonstrations of joy; and as this spot had hitherto been the extent of our visits in this direction, I availed myself of the happy disposition evinced by the inhabitants to press the necessity of their furnishing me with guides for the continuance of our journey. This proposition was met with very little favour; and it was evident to me that a feeling of dread at visiting the natives of Hotset, whose sincerity, even in times of peace, they always mistrust, opposed an effectual barrier to the speedy accomplishment of my wishes. Seeing, therefore, that none of those present were willing to accompany me, and desirous of showing the Indians that we could travel without their assistance, I asked one of the chiefs for verbal directions as to the route, and gave the word for starting again. We now proceeded by land, the canoe and its appendages being left in care of the chief.

Having coasted for some distance along the left bank of the river, the road, which was in some places scarcely traced, struck obliquely up into the interior, in a direction nearly west by south. The country, for the remainder of this day's march, was level, but much obstructed by the abundance of brushwood, and by wind-fallen trees, which in many places impeded our progress. The day following, having passed several diminutive lakes, we began to ascend, and presently came in sight of a high mountain, over which it was evident we should be obliged to pass, though at what precise point was a problem most difficult to solve, as the track which had hitherto guided us, no longer appeared. As this occasioned us all very considerable anxiety, considering the difficulty and danger in which we might immediately be involved by attempting a wrong pass, I ordered a halt, and had breakfast prepared, while some of my most active men went to examine whether there existed on either side of us, any indication of the track usually followed, and from which we might have inadvertently deviated. They had scarcely set out on this errand, before their attention, in common with my own, was arrested by a faint shout, which appeared to proceed from the side of the mountain. Hereupon our scouts returned, & I ordered a couple of shots to be fired as a signal, which were instantly answered by a single one in return. The smoke of the discharge served to indicate the position of our unknown neighbour, and presently after, two human beings were seen cautiously descending the face of the steep declivity, sometimes disappearing among the crannies of the rocks, at others standing in bold relief in the foreground.

The approach of these fortuitous visitors seemed to promise the means of extricating us from our dilemma. They proved to be sheep-hunters, from the vicinity of Nass-chick, who had on several occasions visited Killmaurs, and attracted my regard by the modest propriety of their demeanour, combined with an air of independent confidence by no means common to their associates.

The father of these young men, for they were brothers, was an Indian of the Rocky Mountain Secanny tribe, who had married a woman of the Nataotins. Attached in some degree to the latter by this connection, he had yet at all times maintained the stately independence which characterizes the Secanny, as contrasted with the Babine Indian; or which, in a more extended view, is morally distinctive of the native hunter of the wilds of North America, from the more ignoble fisher of its waters. The parents of his wife had long since paid the debt of nature, and now the only tie which had bound the old man to these strange lands, was dissolved by the death of his partner, which had taken place some months previous to the present rencontre. Thus released from the ungenial society of those who had no claims upon his regard except their connection with his wife, and from the bonds of conjugal affection which had hitherto restrained his wandering propensities, the veteran hunter proposed to himself the abandonment of his adopted country; with a view to rejoining, in company with his two sons, the society of his old friends and relations, if haply they yet roamed amid the wild fastnesses of the Rocky Mountains. In prosecution of this object, he and his sons were now eagerly employed hunting to procure a sufficiency of provisions for a grand feast in memory of his departed wife, and as a valedictory repast to the associates of his married days, to whom, perhaps, he was now about to bid an eternal adieu.

The welcome arrival of these young men removed every difficulty, as they readily agreed to join company with us. After breakfasting, we set forward in good heart, and began ascending the steep acclivity opposed to our progress; a labour, I must add, by no means agreeable, or very rapidly accomplished, as we were compelled to stop from time to time in order to recover breath. Marching or climbing in this painful manner, and envying the comparative facility with which our guides overcame every obstacle, we we were four hours reaching the summit of the mountain. Here I gladly sat down to admire the fine panorama of the country which it afforded. Behind us lay the extensive lake of the Nataotins, its immediate shores fringed with a dark line of pines, while the background offered an agreeable variety of fir-crowned eminences, interspersed with brown, grass-covered hills. The great height of our position afforded a bird's-eye prospect of all the western portion of the lake; its deep indentations lying exposed to the eye as if accurately delineated by the hand of some huge giant, on a chart of dimensions huge enough to be regarded as an exact portraiture of nature.

On our left hand was a chaotic assemblage of mountains, all of them more or less wreathed with snow, which, drifted by the wintry gales among the angular projections of the rocks, had resisted the heats of by-gone summer, and now lay dazzlingly white, as the declining sun cast its weakened rays upon them, causing a *mirage* by which the picturesque effect of the whole was greatly heightened. Our own mountain, for so I shall term the one whereon we stood, bore away the palm, however, for its goodly stature, from all the rest. A lofty pinnacle, whose summit was covered with a venerable crown of eternal snow, reared its head on the right hand of our path, overtopping all the neighbouring heads, like a patriarch of the olden days, standing amidst the crowd of his attendant elders, or like some leaf-crowned monarch of the forest, rising pre-eminently conspicuous over its less noble companions.

Having sufficiently admired the scene, I turned to ask the opinion of my fellow travellers, who, I thought, would at least participate in the delight I felt on beholding it. I had, however, miscalculated on the measure of sympathy to be expected from these Canadian or Indian rovers, for anything wherein beauty and grandeur, however sublime, call for the exercise of the imagination. Three of them were stretched at full length enjoying a doze after the fatigue of the ascent; the rest were unconcernedly smoking, reclined against their bundles; while the two Indians sat stoically puffing their small calumets, inhaling the precious fumes with an indescribable gusto, and again emitting them, after a protracted internal circulation, heaven knows through what intricate channels, like the breath of the war-horse.

Such was the disposition of the forces, and certainly if a stupid indifference to the grandeur or beauty of nature could have entitled its possessor to a premium, each of my companions in arms might have contended for its acquisition. I observed, however, that one of my men, while all the others were either asleep, or idly chatting together, sat silently by, without seeming to regard anything that was seen or done in his presence. He was a Canadian, of Franco-Scottish descent, and, from the sobriety of his character, had been preferred to the situation of body servant to my august self. This man, at least, thought I, seems to enjoy the scene in admiring silence: but here again I was mistaken; his thoughtful reserve proceeding, as will be seen, from another and totally different cause.

"Dormez-vous, Bernard?" said I, in a half jocular way, wishing to ascertain the sentiments of the only one whom I deemed capable of appreciating my own enthusiastic admiration of the scene—"Dormez-vous?"

"Je ne dors pas," replied he, in a serious tone of voice, and in a manner quite different from usual. "Je n'ai pas envie de dormir, vraiment, Monsieur. J'ai de quoi m'occuper l'esprit."

"Bon la—what's in the wind now? You seem low-spirited—surely nothing has happened to disturb your equanimity in this out-of-the-way place."

"Have the kindness," said he, "to continue the march, and I will then, without attracting the notice of my comrades, impart to you, as we go on, the subject which now disturbs me."

I saw that the poor fellow was really attacked with some strange misgiving, and at once accorded his request, desiring him to follow me closely, in order that he might communicate the story which seemed to weigh upon his mind.

Our path lay for some distance along the top of the mountain. A few scattered and shrivelled blades of grass, intermingled with an occasional tuft of a brown weather-beaten-looking plant, somewhat resembling the Scottish heath, were the only indications of vegetable life in these elevated regions. Huge wreaths of snow, from their situation unaffected by the summer sun, filled every cranny on both sides of the ridge along which we were walking; while the long shadow of the snowy peak on our right spread a sombre gloom over the immediate vicinity, strongly contrasted with the lightsome aspect of the unshaded precipices opposite. Before us lay an apparently interminable vista of mountains, rising precipitously from the sides of a deep valley into which we now began our descent.

I was about to remind Bernard Debreuille of his promise, when it suddenly struck me that I had not yet named the mountain, which, as being the most remarkable in the vicinity, and now for the first time traversed by civilized feet, certainly merited some distinction of this sort. I referred to Bernard.

"Call it *Saint Bernard*, Monsieur; it is today the *fête* dedicated to my patron; and, moreover, I will give you good reasons to prefer that name."

"So let it be, my good fellow," said I, laughingly, "be your reasons what they may."

We were interrupted by a shrill whistle not far from us.

"Hist!" said Bernard, firmly closing his lips, and looking intently forward—"Monsieur, je vous en prie ecoutez!"

"Tut, tut!" said I; "Bernard, my good lad, you become childish, leave me alone;" and as I spoke, I withdrew my gun-cover, took aim, and sent a bullet through the brain of the innocent cause of his alarm—a fat marmot which had been curiously peeping at us from the mouth of his hole, and which, from its colour, was scarcely distinguishable from the surrounding rocks. In the neighbourhood, I observed many tracks of these animals, &

the guides informed me that these hills were their usual resort. They appeared to congregate in small colonies, burrowing in the ground, and announcing the approach of danger by the shrill whistle before alluded to. There are two species of these animals, respectively inhabiting the high lands and the low country; both in much esteem as articles of food, and as such, a good deal sought after. They remain confined to their burrows during the whole of the dead season, while fruits and different herbaceous productions are not procurable; and are remarkable beyond other animals for their improvident habits.

The shadows of evening now began to overtake us, and it was necessary to hasten onwards to some spot where water and fuel for the night's consumption might be found. After descending rapidly for about half an hour, we discovered a small spring, issuing from the vicinity of some stunted pines, where we encamped till morning. In the course of our hurried descent, Debreuille accounted for his despondency by explaining to me that his slumbers of the preceding night had been disturbed by dreams, involving the fate of some of his dearest friends; among others, of a young woman, the daughter of a rich Canadian farmer, to whom he was clandestinely betrothed. To crown the whole, Saint Bernard, his patron saint, had appeared to him in a vision, predicting death, and warning him of instant repentance of those sinful deeds which he, in common with other mortals, was daily committing.

Despising superstition as much as any man, I yet saw that this was not a case to be trifled with. It was evident to me that the imagination of the poor man was more than ordinarily affected; and, duly sympathizing with his feelings, I pointed out to him the folly of submitting to the influence of such trivial causes. I endeavoured to convince him that his foreknowledge of the approaching fête-day of his patron saint had given rise to his imaginary visitation, supporting my argument by instancing his ridiculous alarm at the harmless whistling of the marmot, so opposed to his ordinary calmness under circumstances of surprise less childishly trifling than those in question. He admitted the justice of all I said, but it was easy to discover, from his desponding tone of voice, that I had not succeeded in my object, and that the untoward fancies by which his mind was oppressed, yet haunted him. It was still the same through all the next day's march, notwithstanding his own evident desire to conceal his melancholy, and the efforts which I repeatedly renewed to divert his attention. Poor fellow, his was a disease which has baffled the utmost skill of physicians more learned than myself, and the utmost care of how many solicitous and beloved friends!

After traversing the sides of the valley, through which a small rivulet gurgled merrily towards the main stream, whither we were directing our steps, we reached the spot previously designated by the guides, and encamped as before. On the morrow, the sun did not find us lingering; and by noon we arrived on the hills which overlook the romantically situated village of Hotset. It was in all probability owing to the heat of the day that we found all quiet, the only signs of life being a few children, and half a dozen curs, lazily rolling in the grass. A loud whoop from our Indian companions, however, made our approach known, and immediately all was animation; crowds upon crowds of naked savages pouring out of the huts, and clamorously repeating the cry of "netta! netta!" the word expressive of Europeans, by which the quality of their visitors was announced.

Formed into Indian file, myself leading the column, we descended into the plain adjoining the lodges. Of these there were twenty-eight, of large size, each of them affording accommodation, on an average, to six or seven families. The village was divided into two, by the course of the river, which at some distance above and below was of considerable breadth, but at this particular spot was contracted within very narrow limits by steep rocks on either side, rising perpendicularly to a great height, their upper masses overhanging towards each other, and making a fearful chasm, through which the torrent foamed and boiled, as it dashed madly along. Over the narrowest part, where it was not more than forty feet across, lay a huge pine-tree stripped of its branches, which had been felled designedly to form a bridge of communication between the opposite sides. The neighbouring country seemed to consist of a variety of strong wood and prairie, in unequal proportion, the former by far predominating; while in the immediate vicinity of the village were scattered groups of stunted aspens, which contributed to form, on the whole, an engaging prospect.

I had time to cast but a very cursory glance at the general features of the scene, when we were met, on the confines of the village, by the principal inhabitants, headed by their chief, "bearded like the pard," as were a great many of his retainers. The attire of these magnates was ludicrously incongruous, and I had some trouble to suppress a smile as I offered my hand to each in succession, a symbol of which they had learned the meaning from their neighbours of Nass-chick. Accustomed as I had been to the extravagancies of an Indian toilet, I was scarcely prepared to witness such grotesque refinement as I found displayed by the beaux of Hotset, whether they strutted up in gaudy shreds of worn-down finery combined together in the most indescribable confusion of lines and forms, or, less diffuse in their tastes, paced soberly forwards in suits, or half-suits, of shabby genteel vestments which might have graced the purlieus of Monmouth-street. One grim-looking fellow stood eminently conspicuous in a scarlet coat, unaccompanied by that nether appendage which a delicate spectator might have deemed necessary to decorum; while another, his nearest neighbour, rejoiced in a regimental coat of the Sappers and Miners, and the very decorous adjunct of a half-worn pair of corduroy trousers! The whole of these fineries, I must add, by the way, had evidently been assumed for the occasion, as one of great state, and it seemed only charitable to ascribe the little discrepancies I have mentioned to the hurry of their toilet.

It may occasion some surprise that savages who, as I have said, were perfect strangers to the sight of Europeans, should possess so many articles indicative of a commercial intercourse. To explain this, it is only necessary to state that the river affords a communication between these unsophisticated races and the Indians inhabiting the coast and its mouth, known by the name of Chyniseyans. Through this channel, a constant barter of furs in exchange for articles of European merchandize procured from the traders by the Chyniseyans, is carried on, upon a scale of magnificence of which the example cited must suffice.

The ceremony of hand-shaking having been gone through, with a gravity which its novelty, to one party at least, did not fail to secure for it, the chief led the way to his lodge, to reach which it was necessary to cross the primitive bridge I have mentioned. This, to the eyes of the natives, who were accustomed to the feat from their childhood, offered nothing to cause a moment's tremor or apprehension, and it seemed not to enter into their minds that a different view of the subject might be entertained by others. For my own part, I must acknowledge that I felt some repugnance to follow, as they unhesitatingly led the way over the fearful abyss. In order to conceal my hesitation, and gain time to "screw my courage to the sticking place," I turned round, and ordered the men, excepting Baptiste, my interpreter, to re-ascend the hill which overlooked the village on the Killmaurs' side, where I requested them to erect the tent, and await my return. I warned them, at the same time, not to place too much confidence in the integrity of the Indians, and to be ready at a moment's call, should I unhappily require their assistance, to repel treachery; not, however, that I suspected it, but merely to put them on their proper guard, by giving them ground for salutary suspicion. After giving these orders, observing all eyes turned on me, I assumed as much unconcern as I could, and resolutely advanced, like a sick man bent on swallowing a disagreeable draught, to cross the giddy passage. Luckily, it was not more than fifteen paces across, and by keeping my eyes steadily fixed on the opposite shore without allowing them to stray downwards on the rushing stream, I got on much to my own satisfaction, and without betraying any symptom of the awkward feelings of nervousness which I had inwardly experienced. Baptiste followed me closely, and we were presently ushered with great formality into the lodge of Sniggletrum, the *nom de guerre* by which I understood the chief to be distinguished.

Being seated *à la Turque*, on a bear-skin spread for my accommodation, Baptiste stationed on my right hand, and my two Secanny guides, who stuck to me wherever I went, on my left, I had leisure to look about me; Baptiste in the mean time preparing tobacco for a general smoking bout, the usual preliminary to the transaction of all ceremonious business here as elsewhere among the Indians. The lodges, I observed, were built on the same model as the Carrier, though more spacious, and of neater construction; boards split from the cedar-tree forming the sides, instead of the peeled sapling firs used for that purpose by the latter. Some of these boards were of great breadth; one which I subsequently measured was more than four feet, while others which I casually saw, appeared even to exceed that limit. Among other ornaments indicative of a commercial intercourse with the natives of the coast, I noticed a couple of paltry mirrors nearly a foot square, set in deal frames gaudily ornamented with gilt and varnish. On one of the large boards just mentioned also, a brig under full sail was rudely delineated in charcoal and vermillion—the work, as I understood, of one of the Chyniseyan chiefs who periodically come up the river to trade.

According to the Carrier custom, a meal was speedily prepared, and set before me, consisting of a fat beaver boiled, of which, out of compliment to my host, I slightly partook, the remainder being set aside, and afterwards sent to my tent. Our store of tobacco, meanwhile, had come into great request, and the dense cloud of pungent smoke which canopied our heads, gave sensible testimony to the energetic use that was made of it.

Tobacco! By that simple word how many ideas are conjured up! How strange that a weed at first nauseating and unpalatable, and whose effects are confessedly pernicious to the constitution, should obtain such high rank among the choicest luxuries of the human race; and how much more strange that it should have attained this high consideration, and come into universal use, in defiance of the anathemas fulminated against it by ecclesiastical authority, and the decrees of temporal potentates! So it is, however. In the civilized portions of the globe, tobacco forms the principal luxury of the lower classes at large, and the only one of many individuals. At sea, tobacco is the solace of the mariner in his perils, and his comforter in many a dreary watch. In the wilds of America, ask the hardy voyager, ask the rude trapper, ask the dusky savage, from the bleak shores of Labrador to the remote coast of the Pacific, to name his greatest luxury—Tobacco, tobacco, tobacco: this and this only, is the great desideratum. With it in plenty all is well; without it, gloom and dullness instantly prevail.

So it was, that eating and smoking in the present case prepared the way for a good understanding with the chief, to whom I communicated, through the medium of my interpreter, the precise object which led me to visit his lands, expressing, at the same time, a wish to enter into arrangements with him, by which a constant intercourse for purposes of traffic might be established. His answer was favourable to my views, and after a protracted conversation, I left the lodge to return to my men. Before departing, however, presents of furs were made to me by "Sniggletrum," & several of his principal men, which I caused to be transferred to the tent.

Among other articles was one with which, under present circumstances, I would gladly have dispensed. This was nothing else than a young bear, alive, of the red-snouted species, well-known for the savageness of their disposition. When it was presented to me by "Sniggletrum," I was on the point of refusing it, but Baptiste privately whispered me that the bear was the family symbol of the chief, who would not relish any mark of disrespect shown towards it. Thus warned, I thought it best to accept the unwelcome gift, and to dispose of it subsequently as I best could. This ill-omened beast was in the end the cause of much trouble; and when I first saw it dragged forward by a long cord which compassed its neck and one fore-paw, I secretly wished it once more free in its native woods, or anywhere except in my unwilling possession. The perverse brute seemed little inclined to move in the direction required, but struggled and pulled back most strenuously; emitting cries harrowing in the extreme, resembling very nearly those of a young child, so pathetically modulated, that one could almost fancy the poor animal had sense approaching to that of humanity, and was supplicating the mercy of its tormentors. At length, to my momentary satisfaction, the knot gave way, and Bruin availed himself of the accident by making off with himself towards the trees. The tocsin, however, was sounded, and crowds upon crowds of savages set off in pursuit, and after a short chase succeeded in recapturing the runaway. But this was not done without much resistance, so that one tall fellow, of the family of Couthiro, another of the chiefs, had his hand severely lacerated by the teeth of the now infuriate animal. To revenge the injury, he seized an axe, and would have sacrificed the bear on the spot, had the bystanders not prevented him.

For my own part I must acknowledge that I would willingly have seen an end put to further trouble, by the summary infliction of condign punishment, had it not been for the commotion which the very attempt to commit an action so degrading to their family pride at once created among the partisans of the bear. Knives and daggers gleamed forth in an instant, while muskets, and all the minor instruments of war, were hastily assumed by either party, and a collision seemed impending, likely to involve serious consequences. At this juncture, hoping by my interference to quiet the disturbance, and to allay for a time the virulent animosity of the two parties, the explosion of which had been brought on by a cause so trivial, I advanced with Baptiste, through means of whom I essayed the office of a mediator. The yells and shouts of several hundred voices, mingling in harsh dissonance, were gradually reduced to quiet by my appearance—so far, at least, that Baptiste's words could be heard; and after a while it was agreed between the rival parties to relinquish hostile measures, and to unite in rendering my stay among them agreeable.

Meanwhile, the hapless cause of all this commotion, having been secured by a leathern cord, the end of which was fastened round the trunk of a tree, had turned about so often in his endeavours to escape, and so tightened the halter, as I may well call it, considering the catastrophe which it caused, as to strangle himself. I had wit enough to conceal my secret satisfaction, as the brute lay, half-suspended, his tongue lolling out, his eyes starting from their sockets, and his unclosed lips displaying the grinning teeth which seemed only a too faithful caricature of the savage brawl we had just witnessed. His death, since it was evidently accidental, was looked upon without concern; and as there was nothing in the customs of the tribe to prevent the flesh being eaten, I had the carcass sent over to my men, who made a hearty meal of it. Shortly afterwards, I re-crossed the bridge, and ascended to my tent, where I partook of supper, which Bernard had prepared during my absence; and, having posted a couple of sentinels, to be relieved at intervals, slept in broken slumbers till morning.

The next day was occupied in making return presents to the chiefs, trading in furs, and discussing the many topics which presented themselves in the course of conversation; so that it was not till the following morning at sunrise, that I could arrange for setting out on my return. The hour having arrived, I now went to pay a parting visit to the chief; again crossing and re-crossing the rude bridge—a feat which, being by this time in a degree accustomed to, I began to view with less dread than at first. Unhappily, when I returned from this visit of ceremony, I found that I had lost my keys, which I supposed had remained in the lodge where I had been sitting. Calling to one of the men to go in quest of them, Debreuille, though not particularly named, set off on this errand, and, reaching the bridge, appeared to hesitate, but the next moment, as if ashamed of his weakness, hastily crossed over.

Observing how little confidence he had in his footsteps, I called out to him, when he presently returned from the lodge, not to risk the bridge, but to proceed on foot below the fall, and then cross in a canoe. This suggestion he did not adopt, being perhaps afraid of the sarcasms to which it might give rise among his companions; and with much anxiety I saw him again attempt the crossing.

The uneasiness I felt, proceeded from another cause besides the actual unsafeness of the passage; for, since the poor fellow's visionary communication on Mount St. Bernard, I thought I had perceived at intervals, symptoms of insanity in his demeanour, and these, unhappily, had appeared to increase daily. It was, therefore, with feelings highly excited, that I saw him advance dubiously and unassisted, on the frail bridge which alone separated him from eternity; for it is needless to say, that one false step, while in this position, would be instant destruction.

The object of my solicitude seemed, as he slowly and hesitatingly proceeded, to become gradually more agitated by the nervous feelings which few persons have not experienced on similar occasions, and which affect us with such mysterious awe. Whether a friendly voice would have re-assured him at this moment it is impossible to say, for we were afraid of calling out lest the tottering equilibrium which he with difficulty preserved, should at once be destroyed. He had reached the centre of the chasm, and his situation was now indeed critical; his fine form appeared as if spell-bound, so motionless was he; his expressive physiognomy seemed worked to a frenzy of excitement by the tumultuous feelings which agitated him; and, as he gazed downwards on the roaring torrent which rolled beneath him, it seemed as if his every sense were fascinated by some mysterious object, which no one but himself could perceive. Every eye was now fixed on the poor fellow, and a breathless silence reigned among the numerous spectators, which rendered still more awful the rushing din of the cataract, in itself dreadful to contemplate. A poet has written of "darkness visible": to adopt the same idiom of expression, this dread climax of silence was indeed "silence audible." So oppressive did it at length become, that, unable longer to control my feelings, I advanced to the edge of the chasm, and endeavoured, by signs, to attract the attention of the unfortunate man. It was in vain: he stood unmoved and immoveable, still gazing intently as before.

"Debreuille! Bernard!" whispered I. "Bernard!" I called, in a louder voice—"Bernard, look up! Come on, man, for the love of God, come on!"

It seemed for a moment that he had recovered his self-possession, but, as he stared wildly towards me, and stamped his foot impatiently on the tree, I saw that reason, which had so long tottered on her throne, was now completely cast down. The unfortunate maniac seemed no longer to feel giddy or alarmed at his perilous situation.

He gesticulated most fearfully, again and again fixing his eyes intently on the water.

"Bernard!" I again shouted in a loud voice, "come on, I command you!"

He looked up, shrieked out wildly and horribly, uttered some words that seemed to imply recognition, and again relapsed into his state of abstraction.

While endeavouring to invent some means of extricating the man from this perilous situation, my attention was attracted by the most fearful screams I ever heard.

"Oui!" cried the maniac, "oui! je la vois—je la vois; pour la dernier fois, je la vois." And he sprang wildly forwards: "Je la vois, je la vois, je la——"

The sentence was never completed. The unfortunate and hapless-fated individual disappeared for ever in the foaming torrent, leaving the horror-stricken spectators gazing after him, as if able to pierce the dark waste of waters which had swallowed him up.

No vestiges of his body were ever discovered; but, to mark the spot where the sad catastrophe occurred, I caused a rude cross to be erected; a sad memorial of the first visit of Christians to this secluded spot. Our return to Killmaurs was attended with no occurrence worthy of notice; and it was long after reaching home ere I could dismiss from my imagination the fearful cries which had been uttered by poor Debreuille at the closing moment of his existence. Peace to his soul!

Three years after the events I have related, I was passing the winter on furlough in Montreal. Time, which gradually effaces the most vivid impressions, had kindly thrown a veil over the sad memory of my visit to Hotset; and the fate of poor Debreuille, if it ever recurred to mind, was dismissed as hastily as possible. Mixing daily in the sober gaieties of the city, I had little time for the intrusion of melancholy thoughts, and here, if anywhere, I might have expected immunity from them. This, however, was not to be. One day I was invited by a friend to accompany him on a visit to the Chapel of the Hôtel Dieu Convent, to witness the assumption of the veil by a girl whose noviciate had recently expired. It was a grave ceremony, to be sure; but still so interesting, that I hesitated not to accept his invitation, and arm in arm we proceeded to the scene of its performance.

On our arrival, we found the chapel nearly full of people; the rites of the day being then about to commence. The object of the ceremony stood alone, and was remarkable for the air of calm resignation which pervaded her features, in themselves surpassingly lovely, but now seeming of a more elevated order of beauty, from the religious fervour which animated them, as with supernatural light. On a bench in one corner sat an elderly couple, who seemed deeply impressed with the solemnity of the occasion; but more deeply agitated by some internal feeling which they vainly endeavoured to conceal. These were the parents of the novice—of her who was about to sever the dearest ties which connected her with this life — to renounce father and mother for a more mysterious relationship which it might be beyond the power of the poor old people to comprehend.

Mass was performed, and all the imposing rites prescribed by the Church of Rome on similar occasions. The anthem pealed through the aisles, and every studied form was gone through, so well calculated to clothe the broken heart, as with garments of honour. The ceremony was over, and the beautiful Canadian bade a final adieu to the vanities of this world. I felt impelled to inquire her name and history of my friend. "She is the daughter of a rich habitant," replied he —"of him whom you remarked seated in the chapel, and her name is Adèle d'Aubigne." "Enough!" rejoined I: "I know the rest." Need I add that I recognized the heart-stricken lover of the hapless Bernard Debreuille.

PLATE V.

An Indian Hunting Party

CHAPTER VI.

The Bloody Tragedy

O N the evening of the 6th of December we were seated around
our cheerful fireside, "holding sweet converse" on the different
topics of news we had lately received from Canada and England by our overland express, when a loud knocking at the door attracted
the attention of all present, and a Mr. H——, from the Dalles mission, made
his appearance, accompanied by a servant of the Company from Walla
Walla, one of our trading posts on the upper part of the Columbia. They
announced to us the melancholy tidings of the murder of Dr. and Mrs.
Whitman and twelve Americans, with the entire destruction of Wai-let-pu
mission. The following particulars of this bloody tragedy may be relied on.

For some time previous to the massacre, a number of the Cayoux Indians
who resided in the vicinity of the mission, had died of the measles and dys-
entery, which prevailed in every part of the country. The worthy doctor
had been most constant in his attendance on the sufferers, administering
not only medicines, but such other comforts as, indeed, he could ill afford
from his slender stock. Unhappily, his efforts for their relief were vain;
the mortality increased, rather than diminished; and the horrid idea became impressed on the superstitious minds of the Indians, that Dr. Whitman and others had conspired to exterminate them by means of poison!
This idea, however it may have originated, received corroboration, as has

since been ascertained, from the instigations of one Joseph Louis, a Spanish Creole, who for upwards of a year had been employed about the mission in the service of the kind master whom he now sought to destroy. The number of deaths continuing to increase daily, confirmed the diabolical suspicion once entertained, and soon these wretched men resolved on revenging their supposed wrongs, and securing their future safety by murdering all the inmates of the mission.

As the base Creole had urged them to this fatal determination and promised his assistance in the bloody deed, so he was almost the first to commence the tragedy, by murdering two brothers of tender years, the eldest not more than sixteen; a most cruel and cowardly act, for at the time, both lay prostrate on a bed of sickness. The hour of ten in the morning was selected for the butchery, and before many minutes had elapsed, no less than twelve victims had been sacrificed to their wild and revengeful superstition. The first was a tailor, killed on the bench where he was seated at his daily labour; a poor inoffensive being, little suspecting, and perhaps still less prepared, for so awful a change. The next was the worthy doctor himself, who had entirely devoted the last ten years of his life to the instruction of those very savages who were now about to reward him so cruelly. This instruction, I ought to remark, had consisted not only in the principles of Christianity, but in the tillage of the soil, the value of which had long been proved by their abundant harvest. Alas for him, that he had laboured in vain in the culture of their wretched souls; and let us hope that he will meet his reward in heaven!

He was seated at a desk writing when he heard the yell of the murderers, and going to the door, received his first wound. He did not for an instant lose his composure, but calmly returning into the house, drew a chair towards the fire, and sat down, his hands clasped together in prayer, resigned to whatever fate might await him. During this brief interval, the bloody work was going on outside, and the good kind-hearted Mrs. Whitman, who was upstairs, and had rushed to the window on hearing the report of fire-arms, had instantly received, from one wretched miscreant, a ball in her breast. Bleeding profusely, she hastily descended to her husband's room, and, embracing him, began to wipe with her handkerchief the blood that was trickling from his wounds. He fondly returned the caresses of her who, for the last fifteen years, had been the devoted partner of his joys and sorrows in the missionary field, and who in this last dark hour proved herself the same affectionate wife, regardless of her own sufferings, and only thinking of affording relief to her beloved husband. To him what a truly melancholy consolation must the conduct of such a wife have been: she in a dying state herself, yet solely intent upon his comfort! Thus embraced, and perfectly resigned to their fate, the blood-thirsty wretches, armed with guns and axes, rushed into the room, and they were instantly torn asunder never more to meet in this world. The chief, with his axe, so mutilated the face and head of the worthy doctor, that he soon ceased to suffer. The fate of Mrs. Whitman was still more cruel; she was thrown down, and dragged by the hair of her head into the mud, where, with blows and kicks, the inhuman monsters terminated her existence.

The heart sickens at the recital of such horrid brutality, and gladly would I draw a veil over the remainder of the narrative. Let me, at least, relieve it of some portion of its horror, by a few words on the character of the worthy doctor and his amiable wife. Indeed it would be ungenerous in me, having been for many years acquainted with both, were I not to pay a just tribute to their worth. He was, indeed, an honest, upright, and benevolent man; and perhaps there never was one more devoted and zealous in the missionary cause, which had been his study from early years, and was now the sole and constant subject of his thoughts. So anxious was he to prosecute his labours to a successful issue, and so sanguine of at last overcoming all difficulties, that although his health was considerably impaired of late, and he had been warned by the Indians to leave the place, nothing could divert him from his purpose, and much less their threats, which had lately convinced him that those for whom he had made so many sacrifices were capable of rewarding him with a cruel death. Such was the brave-hearted missionary himself; and now, would that my pen could do justice to the character of the good and kind-hearted Mrs. Whitman! In her, it may truly be said, that the orphans found a protector and a mother, for she had no less than nine under her care at this very time; and these she not only educated, but taught the various duties that in after life would prove beneficial and advantageous to them. Often, since this melancholy catastrophe, have I heard these poor creatures deploring, with plenteous tears, the loss of those who had been to them as father and mother. I could say much in illustration of the character of this amiable, and may I add, heroic woman? As a wife, it was her highest delight to anticipate not only the wants of her husband, but of all who visited her hospitable mansion, which pleasure I often had. The last sad scene, however, is the most convincing proof of her fond and devoted attachment to her husband. May we not hope that they will be re-united in heaven? Peace to their memory! they indeed deserved a better fate.

To return to the scene from which these reflections have happily diverted us a short time. The next victim was Dr. Whitman's assistant, who, as several eye-witnesses have alleged, not only implored the Indians to spare him, but acknowledged it was too true that the doctor had administered poison to kill them, thereby confirming all that the base wretch Louis had said, to urge them to these horrid crimes. It is sad to think with what tenacity men will cling to life, and what base expedients they will often resort to in the forlorn hope of preserving it. Although a stranger to me, I am yet confident, from his well-known character, that this unhappy man had no other motive; and if the allegation be true, this subterfuge afforded him only a temporary respite. After making this admission, the savages promised to spare his life, and left him. A few minutes after, however, an Indian, who was at some distance when the promise was made, and was not aware of it, came up with him, and in another moment his earthly career was ended.

While these scenes were enacting, two Americans who had concealed themselves managed to effect their escape—one with his family, consisting of a wife and four children. This little party took the road to the Company's establishment; but the poor woman, having just risen from a bed of sickness, soon became too faint and exhausted to follow; she, therefore, entreated her husband to save her children, and leave her to her fate. As there was a ray of hope that all might be preserved, he carefully concealed her with three of the children in the bushes, and taking one in his arms, succeeded in reaching the fort, a distance of twenty-five miles, in safety. No time was lost by the gentlemen in charge there, in sending relief and assistance to the poor woman; but strange to relate, after a search of two days, the husband despaired of finding her, and concluded that she was lost to him for ever, supposing they had been discovered and murdered by the Indians. He was on the eve of abandoning his search, but a friendly Indian, who had accompanied him from the fort, was far from losing all hope, probably knowing from experience, that if she had been discovered and murdered, some vestiges of the deed would yet be apparent. In short, he renewed the search, and succeeded in finding the now almost lifeless woman, lying concealed with her children in the very spot where they had been left, with scarcely any covering, and without food or fire to keep them warm: in which deplorable state they had now remained four days and nights. The whole party reached the fort in safety, and it is gratifying to add, that the woman, though confined to her bed for some three weeks, was restored to health, and to her friends. The other American escaped by following, in his wounded state, a mark which he struck upon by mere chance, and which led him, by a course of two hundred miles, to the Clearwater mission, where he had never been before, and which he reached after six days and nights travelling, though without food. In these escapes we have additional evidence of the extraordinary exertions and sufferings—in many instances surpassing belief—which the human frame will bear, rather than yield its precious life.

After Mr. Rodgers had fallen, and the two surviving Americans had thus baffled pursuit, or escaped unnoticed, there remained but the now desolate women and children, who had been eye-witnesses of the massacre of their husbands and fathers. The number of these unfortunates exceeded fifty, and my readers must imagine the state of their feelings at the time, and the severity of the trial they underwent. Their lives, indeed, were spared them, but three of the young women were reserved for a more cruel fate, over which I must draw a veil. The other women and children were detained in captivity, and doomed by their cruel masters to toil day and night, until all of them, including the three women above mentioned, were fortunately released, and restored to their friends, with the exception, however, of three children, who had died. During this period—a long interval to them of nearly a month—they were suffering every indignity, and being threatened with death, fear deprived them of their rest. They were at the same time abundantly supplied with food by the Indians, which, indeed, was from their own stock, but they could have easily been deprived of it, and of their lives also. The object of these wretches in detaining them was to procure a ransom, and having their victims so completely in their power, they too well succeeded. Late one evening, the poor captives reached the Company's establishment, strongly guarded by not less than forty Indians, each of whom had some claim to make which dire necessity compelled us to satisfy. Such was the terror and nervous prostration to which they had been reduced, that although every comfort which the slender means of the establishment could supply had been prepared for them, it was many days before they could feel satisfied of their escape from the thraldom of their persecutors.

Another incident worthy of record in this tragical history, was the almost miraculous escape of the Rev. Mr. Spalding, for which, indeed, he was indebted to the timely aid and advice of the Rev. Mr. Brouillet, of the Roman Catholic Mission. The former gentleman was on his return from the Umitalla River, where he had been to visit the sick, and when within a short distance of the mission at Wai-let-pu, where his arrival was hourly expected by the Indians, he was happy enough to meet the Rev. Mr. Brouillet, who had just left the scene of bloodshed. He had gone there, it appears, to administer baptism to two children, and the reader may judge what his surprise, and the state of his feelings must have been to find the bodies of twelve of his fellow-creatures so shockingly mutilated, and lying like dogs in the mud and dirt, with scarcely any covering. With the assistance of his interpreter, he dug one grave for all, and having procured shrouds, he had the satisfaction—and a melancholy one it must have been—of rendering them the last kind office that one mortal owes to another, and which, had they not fortunately gone there, would have been denied by the cruel murderers. Had their remains been exposed one night longer, they would have become a prey to wolves and dogs; but they were now spared this last indignity that could possibly have been inflicted on them.

The Rev. Mr. Brouillet was returning from the performance of this duty, being accompanied by his interpreter, and an Indian, who had evil designs on Mr. Spalding, when they met the latter about six miles from the mission. On this, they all came to a stand, and it required some presence of mind on the part of Mr. Brouillet to warn Mr. Spalding of his danger, without creating any suspicion in the mind of the Indian whereby he would have endangered his own life, without securing his object. He ordered the interpreter to stop and light his pipe; and by the same ruse detained the Indian in the rear to strike fire. The two divines proceeding on in company, Mr. Spalding was soon made acquainted with the particulars of the late occurrence, and strongly advised to escape; his Catholic friend assisting him from his own small stock of provisions. This advice was acted upon in the same haste that it was given: there was no time for deliberation; his life was at stake; and in an instant he left the trail, and proceeded towards the mountains. Mr. Brouillet meanwhile made all despatch to reach his own mission, and when almost within sight of it, the Indian interpreter overtook him. The former, finding Mr. Spalding no longer in company, cast a savage and threatening look on Mr. Brouillet, and immediately retraced his steps in pursuit of his victim. Fortunately, a dense fog, and presently afterwards, the darkness of night coming on, frustrated his evil designs, and thus the life of Mr. Spalding was preserved to his wife & family, whom he rejoined at Clearwater, after wandering for six days and nights among the mountains, losing his horse and provisions, and at last reaching home barefoot.

Would that I might now close this melancholy narrative, but the fate of two Americans stationed at the Grist mill, twenty miles from the mission, must not be omitted. Although six days had elapsed since the destruction of the Wai-let-pu Mission, and more than sufficient time for the ruthless perpetrators of these crimes to have reflected on their enormity, their thirst for blood was unsatisfied. Discovering the forlorn situation of these two men, who were then lying sick and helpless in their beds, the cowards resolved on their destruction, first advancing slowly towards them, lest they should have any weapons of defence at their command. This was not the case; on the contrary, they were implored by both to spare their lives; but mercy was a stranger to their bosoms, and in another instant the assassins uttered a horrid yell, and left the place, their knives and hands covered with the blood of their victims. They were the last who fell in this bloody tragedy.

"Revenge is sweet!" May it fall on them tenfold, for richly do they deserve it! The sole extenuating circumstance, that of being urged on to the commission of their horrid crimes by the bad and ungrateful wretch Louis, can never justify them in so cruelly murdering their benefactor, who had sacrificed his health to promote their happiness in this world, & their hopes of the same boon in the next. Far less would it justify them in numbering among their victims the benevolent Mrs. Whitman and twelve others, who indeed were deserving of a less cruel fate than that which my pen has faithfully recorded.

CHAPTER VII.

The Burning of the Dead

IN the autumn of 1835 I was strolling on the banks of Stuart's Lake, anxiously looking out for the arrival of our annual Canada express, which was now momentarily expected; my thoughts occupied, as may easily be imagined, with many and sometimes sad reflections on the nature of the intelligence that would so soon reach us. Of how many dear relations and friends might not death have deprived me during the lapse of the long year since last I heard of their welfare; and what important changes in the political world might not have taken place, affecting the interests of that country, and of those dear friends, at all times present to the mind of a poor, secluded exile!

The sombre and thick-coming fancies in which I indulged, were suddenly interrupted by a succession of harrowing screams which issued from a neighbouring thicket of pines. Although unarmed, I rushed forward to ascertain the cause; personal security on such an occasion being a secondary consideration, and indeed at all times little regarded by me, who, by placing my trust on Him above, have so often been, I may say miraculously preserved in the many perils I have undergone. I had not penetrated far into the wood, when I unexpectedly found myself in the midst of an assembly consisting of not fewer than a hundred swarthy Indians of both sexes, whose naturally savage countenances presented at this moment, begrimed as they were with a composition of fish-oil and charcoal, an appear-ance more than usually revolting. Guns, axes, and clubs, appeared in the hands of some, while bright daggers glistened, as they moved, from beneath the blankets of others. My surprise at finding myself suddenly in the midst of so rude an assembly was at least equalled by the astonishment evinced by the savages themselves; for, on such occasions as the present, which I speedily discovered to be for the purpose of consuming a dead body by fire, strangers are never invited, and seldom venture to intrude.

Recovering from my momentary surprise, and looking hastily around me, I perceived the corpse of an Indian, a young man of the village, re-cently deceased, stretched on the ground in the midst of a knot of mourn-ers. It was in a state of perfect nudity; and, from the protracted illness which had preceded death, seemed to be reduced to a mere skeleton. Its head was supported on the knees of an individual whom I conjectured to be the widowed wife, although her form was so shrouded by the folds of a ragged blanket, and by the persons of the bystanders, that it was impos-sible to say, with any certainty, even to what sex the sad and silent mourner might belong. Close to the corpse lay a quantity of dry fir; a wood in its very nature inflammable, and in the present instance rendered so in a ten-fold degree by being reduced to thin splinters.

The observation of a few moments had served to make me acquainted with these particulars, and to urge further my curiosity, excited, before now, by the accounts I had heard of the barbarities exercised on these occasions, more especially towards the women. My presence, however, had served to put an effectual stop to their proceedings, and I began to think that the ceremony would be deferred. Unwilling to lose such a fav-ourable opportunity of gratifying my curiosity, I showed no disposition to retire, not even when three elderly men advanced towards me, and inti-mated, in a manner which there was no misunderstanding, their desire that I should do so. I was resolved, in short, unless they should have recourse to force, not to relinquish my position, and therefore made signs that they should proceed with their ceremony, which I had no wish to interrupt.

Upon this they doggedly withdrew, and a vociferous consultation, accompanied with much savage gesticulation, ensued, in which the women bore a prominent part, smothering with their shrill unearthly screams the more deeply intonated cacophany of their lords and masters.

I may remark here that motives of humanity had induced myself, and the other gentlemen stationed in this district, to endeavour all we could to abolish the barbarous practice of burning the dead, which seems to hold its ground more tenaciously in these parts than anywhere else in the interior of the continent. On the north-western coast, indeed, it is still in vogue, but during my residence of five years in that quarter, it was gradually decreasing in frequency; and they had, to my knowledge, on several occasions adopted the European mode of burial. In Western Caledonia, too, to the great benefit of those concerned, the civilized mode of interment is gaining ground, for in 1835, out of eleven deaths which came under my notice, five bodies only were disposed of by burning; and in the two succeeding years three out of five were decently interred. It is here, as elsewhere, with the old people, rather than the younger generation, that most difficulty occurs when practices more congenial with the spirit of humanity are presented for their adoption. The former are most tenacious of their hereditary laws and customs, assigning when urged for a reason, that they are too old to deviate from the path followed by their forefathers. In this, and many other respects, the Carriers are the most superstitious tribe of Indians I ever met with.

But to revert from this digression, and proceed with my revolting narrative. The issue of the noisy consultation among the natives seemed to be favourable to the continuance of the ceremony. The doleful howlings which my appearance had interrupted, recommenced, and I was advised to keep a respectful distance, as the danger of too near approach was imminent. This, however, did not affect my resolution to remain, and I accordingly secured myself a favourable position for witnessing the proceedings.

The near relations of the deceased now commenced erecting the funeral pyre. This was done by laying alternately transverse layers of the split wood before alluded to, till the pile attained the height of about four feet, being at the same time of a corresponding breadth, and more than six feet in length. On the top of the whole was placed the attenuated corpse to be consumed, on which were presently showered down offerings innumerable from the bystanders, in the shape of blankets, shirts, coats, and indeed property of every description, the whole intended as a holocaust, propitiatory of the wandering spirit.

Meanwhile I had an opportunity of more narrowly observing the person and demeanour of the unfortunate widow, for whose sufferings now in prospect, every feeling of sympathy was excited in my mind. She was of youthful appearance, not more than eighteen years of age, and as far as I could judge through the disgusting fucus with which her face was besmeared, comparatively handsome. Her youth, the sorrow, feigned or real, depicted in her features, and the air of resignation exhibited by her whole figure, prepossessed me warmly in her favour, and from my heart I exclaimed,—Alas! poor unfortunate, your troubles commence early in life: may they weigh lightly on you! She advanced, and took her place at the head of the pyre, there to await the progress of events.

It was soon evident to me that every one stood on his guard, for it frequently happens on these occasions that the relations of the deceased revenge his death on some unfortunate being, suspected of being its cause; not by direct agency, but through the mystical power which they ascribe to the object of their suspicion, under the phrase, *being strong in medicine*. These mutual misgivings seemed to increase at the moment when the mother of the defunct advanced towards the pile with a lighted faggot. The screams and gesticulations of the savage crowd redoubled in energy, and all rushed to take, as it were, one parting look at the earthly remains of their countryman. In an instant, the whole pile was in a blaze, and such was the sickening sensation it occasioned to me, that I was almost inclined to withdraw, with my curiosity only half satisfied.

And now, as the flames flickered in fantastic shapes and ghastly colours over the blazing pyre, commenced the sufferings of the poor widowed victim. The husband's relations vied with each other in the infliction of their diabolical tortures, while those of the wife stood silently apart, stoically witnessing the whole scene of barbarity, nor once stretching out a hand to avert a single blow from the poor sufferer. It was with difficulty that I could restrain the ebullition of my feelings, but how much more did I require all my self-command when the poor wretch was flung violently among the flames. She fell backwards, singed and scorched, and only struggled forward into the cool air to be again and again subject to this exquisite torture, and ever at the instigation of her diabolical mother-in-law, who urged her party to the act. While this tragical scene was enacting, the poor wretch was upbraided by her tormentors with fifty imaginary offences against connubial propriety, which, I was afterwards informed, had not the slightest foundation in truth. At length, exhausted with the dreadful tortures to which she had been subjected, their victim fell prostrate and nearly lifeless on the grass, a low moaning sound being the only indication that the spirit had not already departed from its earthly tenement. I was congratulating myself that I had witnessed the last act of cruelty, when suddenly the demoniacal mother-in-law, raised to a perfect frenzy of excitement, seized an axe, and rushing like a fiend on the hapless object of her wrath, inflicted a serious wound on her shoulders. This sudden relapse of malice was more than I could bear, already in a state of feverish excitement from the protracted tortures I had witnessed. Springing forward, I wrested the weapon from the hands of the old woman, whom I flung violently aside. Perhaps it was fortunate for me that vengeance had been fully glutted; no further attempt was now made to injure the unfortunate widow, who lay senseless and bleeding beside the still blazing embers of the pyre.

During the twenty minutes which had been thus fearfully occupied, the body was consumed to ashes. Howlings, screams, lamentations had continued uninterrupted the while, but now every voice was hushed, and all but the nearest relations of the deceased had retired from the spot. These last sat silently eyeing the now dying embers, and when the fire was extinct they collected the ashes and unconsumed fragments of bones, which they carefully wrapped up, and then one by one departed. The widow, helpless, exhausted, as she was, had been left alone on the ground the night through, but her sister humanely kept her company.

By the laws of the Carriers, the widow is made to carry the ashes of her husband until the final inurning, and during this interval, sometimes of two or three years, she remains a slave to his nearest of kin. At her emancipation, when the ashes are disposed of, a grand feast is given, the materials of which are furnished by all the connections of the deceased. This ceremony over, the widow is at liberty to enter the connubial state again should she be so inclined; with the prospect of a repetition of her sufferings hanging *in terrorem* over her head, should it be her lot to undergo a second widowhood.

CHAPTER VIII.

Intermittent Fever

HISTORICAL documents have made us acquainted with the fact that the human race have been afflicted with more or less deadly pestilences from time immemorial; and a perusal of the records which detail the sufferings incidental to some of these supposed testimonials of the divine wrath is inexpressibly harrowing to the feelings. This is more particularly the case—in all probability because we are best acquainted with its circumstances—with that of London in the year 1666, by which some sixty or seventy thousand persons were swept away in a few months, the utmost skill of man, according to the knowledge and experience of the age, being vainly opposed to its ravages. The yellow fever of America, and the plague which continually manifests itself in the Levant, and all along the Grecian Archipelago, would furnish, perhaps, many scenes equally distressing to those who sympathize with the sufferings of their fellow-creatures; while it is well known what deadly havoc has been caused in most parts of the world, by the periodical visits of the cholera morbus. To these and similar instances, I am able to add the following brief memorial of a scene of suffering which came under my own notice a few years ago.

Returning to Fort Vancouver on the Columbia, after a short absence in the autumn of 1830, I found a few of the servants suffering under an attack of intermittent fever. Two medical men being resident there at the time, its first appearance caused no serious apprehension to those in health. But some alarm began to arise when it was found that, instead of disappearing before the remedies applied, the malady fast increased both in virulence and extent. In twenty days after the first symptoms of its appearance, the whole garrison, with the exception of two, amounting in all to five gentlemen and eighty servants, had successively undergone the ordeal, and still remained subject to the influence of this pestilential fever. Those who remained in health were, of course, unable to attend properly to so many invalids, and this increased the inconvenience under which both men and officers suffered in common. The annual ship soon after arrived from London, bringing a seasonable supply of medicines, the recent demand for bark and other tonics having speedily exhausted the limited stock we possessed. Other assistance it was soon out of their power to render us, the new comers being presently attacked in a similar manner to ourselves, and confined with a single exception to their beds. The sufferings of all under these circumstances were necessarily severe, and attended with much serious inconvenience; yet thanks to the remedies thus provided us, and other wise measures by which the virulence of the disease was mitigated, few deaths occurred in the garrison.

Such was the visitation as we experienced it; but with the native population, alas! the case was different. Who shall describe the sufferings of these unsophisticated children of the wilderness; or who depict the forlorn condition they exhibited while subject to such a scourge? Let others, if they will, essay the task; for myself I despair of doing it justice, though the scene is imprinted on my memory with a distinctness which actual observation alone could communicate. A few words, however, may serve as a memento of this sad event, however inadequate to express its fearful reality.

In close contiguity with our clearances was a village containing about sixty families of Indians; a few miles lower down was a second, of at least equal population. These villages, before the fell visitation I have mentioned, resounded with the hum of voices; smiling on the shores of the magnificent Columbia, they refreshed the eyes of the lone traveller, wear-

ied with the unbroken monotony of woods and waters, in the same measure as the bright strand of a newly discovered island raises the sinking
spirits of some forlorn wanderer on the deep. Here, if the wayfarer could
not command the artificial comforts of the European hostel, the wants of
nature were at least cheerfully supplied; and the hireling smiles of mine
host, easily forgotten in the cheer of an Indian welcome! In this sequestered spot, seated on some rude turfy knoll, was it matter of pleasant con-
templation to witness the evening pastimes of the simple villagers. The
lively gambols of the children; the more stirring games of the youths; the
sober gravity of manhood, and the doting garrulity of old age; *human
nature*, in short, here as elsewhere, affected the hearts of all who were not
callous to these finer impressions.

Such was the scene I had often witnessed when visiting these hamlets.
A short month had passed away; the shadow of death on the wing had
just fallen upon our little community, and passed by; and now, as I drew
near the well-remembered lodges, how different were the feelings I experienced! All, all was changed. Silence reigned where erst the din of population resounded loud and lively. No voice of young or old to awake the
echoes of the neighbouring woods. Alas! where are they who not long
since peopled this deserted spot? Where are they disappeared? Let these
unburied carcasses resolve the question; these torn and mangled corpses,
say wherefore. Why linger those foul birds around the spot, gorged, and
scarcely noticing my presence?—yon wolf, who eyes askant the wretched
scene, and revels in the ideal enjoyment of his interrupted banquet? The
death-like silence around me, the fell vestiges of a sad calamity which I
descry—the loathsome remains of mortality which alone indicate what was
once the scene of life and vigour—are my only answer. These speak louder
than words, more than volumes; they tell me with awful distinctness that
here, where the voice of laughter, and the rude Indian chant, have so often
made my heart glad, the fever-ghoul has wreaked his most dire vengeance;
to the utter destruction of every human inhabitant.

It may be inquired how such fatal effects arose from a cause not generally productive of them. This may be easily accounted for in the trust

which these poor, deluded savages reposed in the juggling mountebanks with whom the science therapeutic solely rests among them; and their total neglect of the precautions that were recommended by us for their adoption. Maddened by fever, they would rush headlong into the cooling stream, where, in search of relief, they found only the germs of dissolution.

Dreading lest the putrified remains of the dead should occasion some more dreadful pestilence, we proceeded forthwith to remove them. But, as this would have been a work of much labour, besides being inexpressibly disgusting, it was resolved to consume them by the most purifying of all elements. Accordingly, they were collected in heaps, and the whole point of wood where they lay set on fire. Upon this occasion one poor old man who had retired among the branches to repose himself—probably the only survivor of all the inhabitants of the nearest village—narrowly escaped a more cruel death than his friends and kinsmen. Too weak to extricate himself from the wood, it was only by his cries that we learned the fact of his existence, and could discover the spot where he was concealed. Though preserved from a fate which it is dreadful to contemplate, his life had only a short respite; for, on the morrow, wasted to death through neglect and sickness, he breathed his last. This was the last case of a fatal nature which fell under my notice, and certainly the measure of horror was full to the brim, and without any further addition to cause its overflow.

It was not till the month of November that the symptoms which incommoded the garrison began to abate, and another month elapsed ere they had entirely disappeared. They have since occasionally manifested themselves among the whites, as well as the native population of the lower villages; but the result has never been so fatal as the first appearance of the fever. Much inconvenience, however, arises from it; and I may instance the case of a party under Mr. W——, who were attacked by this disease on their way from the Rio Sacramento, when two of his men fell victims to it, and the remainder with difficulty reached Fort Vancouver, and that only after assistance, both of men and medicines, had been sent to them. Two years previously I had myself visited the Sacramento, but saw nothing of any general sickness. Mr. W——, however, had found the intermittent

fever raging among the natives; and, seeing that his whole party underwent its ordeal, it was in one respect a fortunate circumstance that it was
not confined to them, since, had the natives been in their wonted good
health, it is probable that an expedition thus weakened would have fallen
a sacrifice to their vindictive treachery.

It is a question of some interest where this epidemic had its first origin;
and upon the whole I have little doubt that it came from the direction of
the Spanish settlements; for, in the country north of the Columbia, it has
hitherto not made its appearance; though still flickering about the lower
parts of that river. To suppose it contagious from personal contact would
be very erroneous, since it doubtless proceeds from miasmata pervading
the atmosphere, whose virulent qualities are elicited only by certain coin-
cident circumstances of local origin.

After all, perhaps, the most plausible mode of accounting for the generation of this malady is, to attribute it entirely to foul exhalations from
low and humid situations; though even to this supposition there are objec-
tions which it is difficult to overcome, and which tend to subvert every
preconceived theory on the subject.

CHAPTER IX.

A Western Caledonian Feast

THE native village of Stellah is situated some twenty miles from our establishment, at the west end of Frazer's Lake, by the confluence of a stream which flows into it at this spot from the French Lake. Here, at the repeated solicitation of Hanayah, the Carrier chief, I consented to grace a festival which he was about to give to his friends and neighbours, with my own lordly presence. Though hardly persuaded to this act of condescension, I may whisper in the reader's ear that Hanayah's request had in reality coincided with my own inclinations from the first: my desire being to acquire a more intimate knowledge of our rude neighbours from their living manners. I had feigned reluctance, however, in order to enhance the merit of complying with the chief's wishes.

I shall attempt to describe what I witnessed on this occasion, with as much accuracy as the impression left on my mind will permit, first introducing to my reader's acquaintance, the prime genius of the whole affair, my worthy host, Mr. Hanayah. A little fellow, some four feet ten inches in height, of spare make, and bearing on the whole a marvellous resemblance to that caricature of our species, an ape, will hardly come up to the idea he has probably formed of an Indian chief in his own wilderness; yet I cannot be guilty of the gross flattery to describe him otherwise. Endow this little comicality with a dash of good humour, and the extra measure of self-conceit which Dame Nature kindly allows to little people in other climates besides this—in order, perhaps, to eke out their stature—and you have a pretty correct idea of the promoter and leader of these intended revels.

But contemptible as may be the opinion which a mere personal description of this man must create, it were unfair to deny him the merit of maintaining a very rigid authority among his people. To obtain as well as to preserve this influence, Hanayah had adopted the plan of a most arbitrary sovereign, and addressed himself rather to the fears than to the love of his subjects; but with this important difference from his civilized prototypes, that his means of exciting dread were impalpable. Conscious enough that he could not boast of an "eye like Mars to threaten and command," he wisely eschewed any pretensions to the character of a brave, for on this score he would have found plenty of competitors to dispute the palm of superiority. Like a skilful general, he went more cunningly to work, and by aiming at the superstition of his followers, secured for himself exactly that kind of respect which once on a time, had he lived in enlightened England, would have gained him the compliment of a faggot and a tar-barrel. This good man, in short, possessed the attribute of the "evil eye" in all its perfection; was moreover a seer of undoubted pretensions; and could utter oracles like the Delphian Apollo. Is it any wonder that Hanayah, with such transcendant qualities, obtained the influence which is justly allowed them in more polished communities?

Despatching my tent and other necessaries in a canoe, I rode to the scene of festivity on horseback, attended by my interpreters, and found a large concourse of Indians encamped among the trees. Some of these were from Nautlais, others from the Babine's Lake, and not a few from the borders of Simpson's River—downright scamps, these last, and unattached to us by the same commercial ties which secured the good-will of the rest. I was made welcome with a fat beaver and some berries, set before me in the lodge of my entertainer. This was a spacious building, perhaps forty feet square, having a small door at one end, and the ridge of the roof being left uncovered to permit the egress of the smoke. Four posts, carved with grotesque figures, supported the double ridge-trees upon which the roofing-sticks rested; and a thick covering of pine-bark effectually excluded the heaviest showers. The sides of the building were formed with broad boards split from the pine-trees, but no care was taken to join them, or even to fix them solidly; so that the large interstices allowed free ingress to the air—a circumstance the less considered, as the building was merely appropriated for summer use. A general cleaning up had evidently taken place in anticipation of the usual concourse of guests; and saving a few bundles of property and utensils pitched against the sides of the building, it exhibited none of the ordinary signs of habitation.

The feast was appointed to begin the next morning, and, as my tent had meanwhile been pitched, I retired to it, and was shortly visited there by the whole body, gentle and simple, of the assembled crowd. A few feet of tobacco cut up and distributed, afforded a general smoke, after which the rude levee retired, and left me to my own reflections. I slept little during the night, for the company assembled in the vicinity, by groups of twenty or thirty together, kept up an incessant uproar till daylight. In fact, each of these assemblies maintained a gambling table, where all the passions exhibited in the polite *hells* of St. James's were exemplified in a more barbarous and no less energetic manner. For some time I amused myslf with the observation of their motions from a distance. The little fires by which they sat, were kept continually blazing, and the light thus afforded enabled me to distinguish the gestures of the players without difficulty; the run of "luck" and the changing passions of those engaged, being often indicated by the violence of their gesticulations, aided by a more emphatic intonation of their wild song. Some disputes occasionally arose, which threatened serious quarrels, but they were invariably arranged, after much vociferous altercation, without leading the disputants to extremities.

I cannot help remarking, by way of parenthesis, on that indomitable passion for play which prevails among the aborigines of this continent, & its singular coincidence with the same propensity among polished nations. The universal prevalence of this vice among the natives, the excesses to which it sometimes leads, the misery it causes, the unconquerable hold it maintains upon the deluded wretch who has once indulged in it, are as deplorable in the one case as the other. The trader far away from home, in pity of the uninstructed, unsophisticated, and half-naked savages of America, is induced for a moment to lament their want of the civilized education of Europe when he beholds them engaged in these degrading orgies. Alas! the next instant he is only humiliated by the remembrance of similar scenes in the most refined society. Go, visit the magnificent temples of Mammon in St. James's, or shift the scene to Paris, to Amsterdam, or any other of the capitals of Europe, and shall we not there find, despite of book-learning and all the vaunted influences of civilization, as much eagerness for the gains of this detestable vice, as in the comfortless lodge of the most barbarous savage? Sad to think, it has its foundation in the worst feelings of our nature, for its indulgence must invariably occasion as much distress to the one party, as exultation to the other. Selfishness—every gradation, in short, of meanness—is developed and personified in this one accursed vice of our common nature.

But I am digressing from my story, and must either renounce such disquisitions or leave my tale unfinished. After I had breakfasted, of course in my own tent, Hanayah came to usher me to his lodge, where the native guests were already assembled. I was placed in a position which commanded a view of the whole assembly, my interpreter being accommodated near me. The other guests were seated on the ground, in rows, back to back, and, with the exception of the vacancies preserved between the rows, occupied the whole area of the lodge. There were, perhaps, two hundred present. Huge piles of dried meats, with vessels of bear's-grease and fish-oil, besides quantities of berry-cakes, were stowed up in the vacant places, so as to leave barely room to pass and re-pass.

At length, the important business of the day commenced; and even to me, who, from constant intercourse with the Indians, had learned to conquer in some degree the delicacy acquired during my youth, it was a most disgusting exhibition. By way of commencement, Hanayah advanced and laid before me a beaver. He then returned to his heap; and, seizing another in both hands, advanced to the most dignified of his native guests, and squatting down, presented it to him, tail foremost. Upon this, the honoured individual seized a knife, and commenced forthwith an attack upon the proffered morsel, which the chief continued to hold with exemplary patience till the guest had satisfied for the time his voracity. The animal, thus despoiled of his fair proportions, was presented to another and yet another of the guests, the allotted portion always diminishing with the rank or consideration in which he might be held. When all were thus served, a new course, attended with the like ceremonies, at once began; and so on till all the provisions were exhausted. About a dozen of his relations, all tributaries to the feast, assisted the head man in the distribution of the viands, the like etiquette being scrupulously observed by the whole. As the banquet proceeded, I observed that the guests, without one decent exception, had amassed a large heap of meats, all tossed "higgledy-piggledy" into their dishes, together with a heterogeneous compound of berries, bear's-grease and fish-oil. I mention these distinctions, but it is quite clear they regarded everything as fish that came to their nets. An utter contempt of cleanliness prevailed on all hands, and it was revolting to witness their voracious endeavours to surpass each other in the gluttonous contest.

When the stock of provisions was drawing to a close, a circumstance occurred strikingly illustrative of the brutish gluttony which may almost be said to form a distinctive mark of the Carriers. Hanayah, filling a large dish with bear's oil, placed it before a Nautlay Indian, named Kusmalah, saying, "Drink this." From the tone of his expression, I saw he was displeased, and was at a loss to conjecture the cause; but it was soon explained.

"Wherefore this?" said his surprised guest.

"Who accused me last winter of eating all my store of grease?" rejoined Hanayah; "I have at least enough left to give you a surfeit. Drink, drink! I insist upon it."

Poor Kusmalah, the "observed of all observers," reluctantly endeavoured to comply, but nature was unequal to the task; and after swallowing about one-half the contents of the dish, he was constrained to set it down. He then stripped off his coat and threw it to Hanayah, thus purchasing exemption from the further exaction of this strange penalty against evil-speaking.

The same plan was adopted, with similar results, in another instance;

and it appears to be a standard maxim of Carrier etiquette thus to punish backsliders from the truth, in affairs such as the present. Need I say more to illustrate—

"The feast of reason and the flow of soul"

in which I was such an envied partaker of this stately banquet?

As the day was far advanced before the company separated, and the ceremony of distributing the presents was deferred till the morrow, I retired to my tent, resolved on waiting another night to witness the conclusion of the festival. Shortly after dark, I heard a great tumult in the chief's lodge, and was informed that the natives, of whom a large party had assembled there, were quarrelling. As blood is frequently shed at these meetings, when the hereditary jealousies of neighbouring septs and families are sure to manifest themselves, I deemed it right to visit the scene of dispute, and, if possible, to quell it. Summoning my interpreter, and taking my sword in case of need, I proceeded to the lodge. There was a large assemblage of Indians, most of whom were standing under arms, and eyeing each other with an air of mutual defiance, while the wordy war maintained between the rival parties bade fair to exasperate their feelings to the utmost extremity. Seated upon the ground, in the midst of the lodge, was Hanayah, togther with two other craftsmen of the same art. Each of them wore a kind of coronet formed of the inverted claws of the grizzly bear, strung together in a circle, the badge of the supernatural powers to which they aspired. These worthies had been engaged in the exercise of the black art, as they professed it, doubtless, to their mutual edification, if not to the satisfaction of their followers; and it was in the course of their dark proceedings that the disagreement had arisen: a spectator, in short, having roundly accused one of the learned trio of causing the death of his father, an old man of fourscore years recently deceased, through the pure decay of nature. This was the prime cause of the disturbance; and, having first drawn attention to my presence, upon these hints I spoke. To be brief, I gave them a round scolding, and rated the whole of them soundly, not even excepting the potent Hanayah himself. The desired effect being attained, I then removed to my tent, and threw myself down till the morning, undisturbed by aught save the musquitoes, which abound in summertime.

The distribution of the presents next morning was prefaced by a ceremony to which much importance was attached. This was the production of such relics of the several defunct members of Hanayah's family as the piety of their relations had preserved, and which were now to be consigned to the flames. These were exhibited by the chief, each in turn, to the spectators, while a passing mention was made of their departed owners. Pots, pans, knives, locks of hair—any, the most insignificant trifle in fact—served to recall the memory of its one-time beloved possessor; and as each trifling memorial was produced, it was affecting to hear the low murmuring plaint which arose from mothers, from fathers, or from children, as the departed objects of their affection seemed once more to speak to their hearts. Be the other attributes of the feast low and unamiable as they may, the exhibition of this simple outbreak of natural affection is yet hallowed in my memory, and there, I trust it will always remain enshrined with all that is worthiest of human sympathy. It is a gratification deep beyond measure to witness among rude beings such as these, the excitement of those pure feelings of our nature which remind us of our common origin, and which, with ties indissoluble in all ages and in all climates, still bind man to man.

The distribution of the presents occupied but a short time. These consisted of blankets, guns, kettles, capots, and other articles of trade; of which every one present at the feast received his due share, that of the great men exceeding their inferiors in the proportion of six or eight to one. For my own part, in order to comply with the established etiquette, I accepted a necklace of shells, valued among the Indians at the rate of a large blanket, in return for which I took care to make over to Hanayah other articles more than equivalent to what I received. In the course of the distribution the number of blankets given by each was accurately counted, and Hanayah's proportion amounted to fifty distinct articles. This ceremony ended, a general rout ensued; each departing on his way without an instant's delay. The native canoes might now be seen setting off in all directions: in ten minutes afterwards not a stranger was left on the ground.

After a pleasant ride homewards I arrived at the fort, not too favourably impressed with the delicacy of Carrier etiquette, but on the whole gratified with what I had witnessed, and revolving in my mind the strange inconsistencies of the world, whether displayed in the saloons of a prince or the rude cabin of a North American savage in Western Caledonia.

CHAPTER X.

The Great Dalles of the Columbia

A MONG the innumerable streams which intersect the American continent, and afford the adventurous trader the means of a precarious intercourse with its remoter regions, the Columbia is pre-eminently conspicuous; not only as being one of the most important rivers on the western side, but likewise for the perils that attend its navigation beyond a certain distance from the ocean. Meandering through a desert region, often rendered more wild and picturesque by the rude vestiges of ancient volcanic action which abound in it, the stream is frequently interrupted in its peaceful course; rushing along in impetuous torrents over the detached masses, or continued ridges of volcanic rock by which its bed is obstructed. Of these rapids one of the most dreaded at certain periods, is the Dalles; distant about 160 miles from the sea, and so called by the Canadian voyager, in common with other places, where a stream is straitened in by steep rocks, so as to create a lengthened torrent of narrow limits, but fearful strength and rapidity. In this particular place the river is parted into a number of channels, separated from each other by insulated tongues of rock, which rise abruptly from the surface of the waters. Some of these channels are navigable, though with great risk even to the most expert boatmen, at certain periods of the year: but in the summer season, when the melting of the mountain snows have swelled the flood beyond its accustomed limits, most of them become undistinguishably blended together, and the mighty waters roll along with irresistible fury. When this occurs, even the most daring quail before the perils of the navigation, and in fact all enterprise of the kind is then considered at an end. It may be supposed that the scene on such occasions is indescribably majestic in its character. The mighty torrent twirls, leaps, and rebounds, as the rocky islets I have alluded to, oppose its progress; while occasionally, as if by some instinctive impulse, a sudden swell from behind, comes fairly breaking over the half-checked waves before it, as if impatient of their dilatory and indecisive progress. Along the shores, on every advancing point of rock, the native fishermen station themselves, sweeping the eddies with light ingeniously wrought scoop nets, and thus speedily procuring an ample supply of the bright scaled salmon as they ascend. Seals, attracted thither by the ascending shoals, swim triumphantly among the whirlpools and eddies, at the lower part; sometimes floating supinely, with their heads above the billows, and again darting to and fro, either in sport, or while pursuing their scaly victims, with admirable velocity.

It was in the summer of 1830 that I arrived at the Dalles on my return to Vancouver, after an absence of eleven months, spent in scouring the prairies in quest of beaver. I had a small party of trappers under my command, and having left our horses at Walla Walla, where a crazy boat had been furnished us, we had reached thus far on our descent, without an accident of any moment, and in eager anticipation of a speedy restoration to our friends. Exhilarated by such a prospect, the natural vivacity of the Canadian voyageurs, increased to ten times its usual vigour—

"From morn till noon, from noon to dewy eve,"
the paddle song echoed over the stillness of the swiftly gliding stream, and now that necessity forced a "portage" on them, the active crew speedily overcame the obstacle, and the boat again floated in safety below. The heat was intense; and though the breakfast hour was gone by, the stench of putrifying salmon was so overpowering, that I resolved on proceeding a few miles lower down, before taking my morning repast. Accordingly, the men were directed to push off and prepare for this important event of the day, at a spot indicated, while I resolved to saunter downward by land. Little did I then anticipate the sequel. Scarcely had I set out, when the

men put forth, and began steering in an oblique direction across the stream in order to avoid a string of whirlpools that for a short distance impeded the direct navigation; and as the boat shot majestically onwards, I half repented my resolution of walking, envying the swan-like ease with which she appeared to descend, so contrasted with my own fatiguing progress. Suddenly, however, the way of the boat was checked; so abruptly, too, that the rowers were nearly thrown from their seats. Recovering their equilibrium, they bent to their oars with redoubled energy, but the craft yielded nought to their endeavours. The incipient gyrations of a huge whirlpool at the same instant began to be felt, holding the boat within its influence. The vortex was rapidly forming, and the air was filled with a confused murmur, high above which might be heard the hoarse voice of the bowsman, shouting, "*Ramez, ramez, ou nous sommes pais!*" The danger became momentarily more imminent; there was no longer any doubt of the sad mischance which had befallen them, for yielding to its fatal attraction, the boat glided, at first slowly, into the whirling vortex; its prow rising fearfully as the pitiless waters hurried it round with increasing velocity.

Is it surprising that I grew dizzy and faint as I gazed, until at length one wild, long cry warned me that all was over, and suddenly restored my senses to their activity? Alas! to what purpose, save an overpowering sense of grief, was the restoration of my faculties of thought!

Utterly incapable of rendering assistance to my drowning companions, I stood a helpless spectator of the scene. The spot where the boat had disappeared, no longer offered any mark whereby to note the sad catastrophe that had even now occurred there, the vortex was filled up, and its very site was no longer distinguishable; for a while it was more like a dream than a real occurrence, so little vestige appeared of the life-struggles which had just taken place. A few moments more, and the paddles, sitting-poles, and various other articles of a buoyant nature, were cast up in all directions around, while here and there, a struggling victim was discoverable, hopelessly endeavouring to evade the fate that awaited him. One by one they disappeared, drawn down by the lesser vortices that continually formed, and again as speedily filled up, in the environs of the catastrophe. After a brief interval, nought was to be distinguished but the now mournful rushing of the waters, and I sat down with the consciousness of being left, in the fullest sense, alone.

At the time, I dared not hope that even one of my unfortunate companions had escaped; but it eventually proved that one of them, poor Baptiste, the steersman, had that good fortune. By seizing four empty kegs, lashed together, according to our mode of transport, the buoyancy of these vessels had floated him off, and the Indians picked him up some miles below the scene of the misfortune. For his companions, it was only after long intervals that the corpse of one or another was occasionally found lying far away along the beach, whither it had drifted with the descending current, and at length been cast by its capricious eddies.

Since then, twelve years have elapsed. Near the spot where I witnessed this sad event, there now stands a humble edifice, rearing its lowly roof above the stunted oaks around it, and environed with several small enclosures where the arid soil of the locality has been subjected to a partial tillage. This little homestead is a station of the American Wesleyan Society, whose missionaries have been established there since the year 1837, with the view of Christianizing the savage residents of the vicinity. Still numerous, these last have yet decreased sadly in numbers, since the date of my story. What may be the ultimate fate of the rest, it is not for blind mortals to foresee; suffice it to say, that their present condition is such as to enlist our warmest sympathy. To one boasting even the shadow of a philanthropic spirit, it is impossible to witness the state of these poor people without experiencing a heartfelt pang of pity, and cherishing an earnest wish that something may ere long be done to ameliorate their sad moral condition.

A few remarks may not be out of place in this connection concerning the most effectual means of persuading the savage mind to embrace the pure doctrines of Christianity. That there are, in fact, certain agencies whereby this end may be accomplished, more practical, and therefore more promising than the advocacy in the first place of a systematic theology, is a position which I assume as too firmly established to require any comment; although confessedly at variance with the persuasion of a religious body,

signalized for their fervent piety, and the zeal with which they seek to dis-
seminate the seeds of gospel truth among the nations. It is impossible not
to admire the untiring energy of this widely-spread sect in such a cause.
But, alas! the best intentions of these good people are frustrated for the
most part by the self-reliance to which I have alluded, causing them to
reject the employment of those intermediate means of conversion, which,
like tillage applied to the soil, are often absolutely necessary to prepare
uncultivated minds for the reception of the good seed. Without some co-
operating influence, whereby the dormant energies of the mind and body
shall be awakened to activity, it is, I fear, but a hopeless task to inculcate
those pure precepts of morality which are co-existent with, and dependent
on, a state of civilization, partial, of course, in the beginning, but of increasing breath as it proceeds, and of greater depth as it extends itself. The
influence of Christianity can never really be felt except commensurately
with the advancement of knowledge, as, indeed, knowledge is of little
avail without Christian virtue; each reciprocally promoting the strength
of the other, in an ever-increasing ratio of progress.

To instance the erroneous views sometimes insisted on, with regard to
this particular subject, I may mention the custom of estimating the missionary, in this particular spot, by the number of *communicants*, without
considering their sincerity, or demanding any further qualification than
their formal acquiescence in a creed or ceremony, whose outward form is
alone adopted; while, it may be, the whole daily conduct is utterly at variance with its evangelical spirit. As a proof that this is often the case, I may
here relate what came under my own observation when re-passing the
scene of my mishap already related, on my way into Western Caledonia
so lately as last summer.

It so chanced, on this occasion, that I encamped at the Dalles and passed
the Sabbath there. An hour or two before noon, Mr. P——, the resident
missionary, made his appearance in the camp, ringing a small hand-bell as
he proceeded to the principal lodge, by way of summons to those desirous
of attending morning service. A goodly concourse was soon assembled,
whose outward decorum was in general unexceptionable; in whom, how-

ever, candour compels me to remark, I could discover no symptoms of that inward change which common report had led me to expect. Among the congregation, my companion, Mr. D——, a Catholic priest who accompanied me on my way up the river, likewise attended. As the service proceeded, we observed in one corner of the lodge a young man, lying there in the last stage of consumption, his brother, a youth of about eighteen, seated by his side. After a brief interval, the attention of every one was aroused by the announcement that the spirit of the sick man had departed; and with the ferocity of a tiger his brother sprang upon a decrepit old woman who sat listening to the preacher's discourse. Before a hand could move to her succour, the infuriated savage had severed her head from the body. A thrill of horror transfixed the civilized portion of the assembly, but they could only execrate the deed they had not been able to prevent. As for the rest, they excused the bloody act of their countryman upon the usual plea — that it was through the evil incantations of the poor victim that the deceased had undergone a lingering disease, terminating in his death as just witnessed. Yet these men had been, and still are, represented as *evangelized* in an eminent degree.

The occurrence I have related is but a type of a thousand atrocities daily occurring among these supposed converts to the merciful precepts of Christianity. Were it an isolated instance, I should be disinclined to advance it as an argument for or against a general proposition; and I merely bring it forward to show how mistaken are the views of those benevolent enthusiasts, who are prone to exaggerate the most distant shadow of success into the fullest confirmation of all the most sanguine hopes that may be entertained by their supporters. As for the belief in sorcery itself, these benighted heathens are less to be ridiculed and blamed than our own countrymen of a past generation, whose infatuated belief in the worst horrors of witchcraft led them into excesses ten times more horrible than this unprovoked murder. And, surely, when these deeds come eventually to be judged at that tribunal where we must all appear, the irregular impulse of the savage breast will plead for extenuation far more efficaciously than the systematic barbarities of those blind credulists, who have "loved darkness rather than light, because their deeds are evil!"

CHAPTER XI.

The Unfortunate Daughter

SELDOM or never has it fallen to my lot, during my protracted residence in these savage wilds, to witness occurrences so tragic as I am about to relate, and in which I was so deeply interested in consequence of a previous acquaintance with the parties. Scenes of violence, indeed, as many of these sketches bear witness, and incidents of romantic adventure, have been of frequent occurrence in my experience; but these circumstances may properly be called tragical, not merely from the violence in which they result, but from the harrowing feelings excited by them, and the dramatic shape in which they address the imagination.

The heroine of my story, was the daughter of a couple, both of native extraction, who resided as inmates of my establishment.

The character of the father, who was somewhat advanced in years, was base and treacherous to a degree; and though, generally speaking, a fond parent, he was possessed of no other redeeming quality, notwithstanding the good advice so lavishly bestowed upon him. He was respected, indeed, because dreaded, by the natives around, who well knew that, once excited, he would hesitate at no crime, to accomplish whatever end he might have in view. The mother's character, on the contrary, was so much the opposite of this, that its delineation, though ever so briefly, is indeed to me a pleasing relief. During the long period of her connubial probation, she had lived respected and admired—enduring with patience the slights and injuries to which her graceless partner continually subjected her, and using every endeavour and straining every nerve to bring up a numerous family with propriety.

Such were the parents; and it cannot be a subject of much wonder if the child of this ill-assorted couple should exhibit a wayward disposition. Notwithstanding a kind mother's constant care, the evil example and immoral habits of her father, had doubtless implanted in her mind the seeds of that evil which eventually ripened into such pernicious fruit. In appearance, she was tall and good-looking, with a complexion savouring of the brunette, eyes of jet black, and a figure every way prepossessing. Her hand had been frequently sought in marriage; but the old man, preferring to see her united with one of his own descent, selected at length him, whom I shall now introduce to my reader's notice.

The son of a respectable Indian trader, he had been sent, while yet a child, to Canada, and there placed under the care of a clergyman, who, I am confident, did ample justice to his charge. This is the plan frequently adopted by Indian traders; but not unseldom, after a lavish expenditure of money, and the most anxious solicitude, they are doomed to see every hope blighted, and to learn, too late, that they have laboured in vain. Others, more fortunate, have reason eventually to congratulate themselves, on seeing their children become efficient and respectable members of society, fulfilling admirably the most cherished duties of life. Let it suffice to say, that he of whom I now speak was not of the latter number. As regards his conjugal relations, I shall only remark that he exhibited at all times a disposition extremely jealous, treated his wife with incessant rigour, and in other respects afforded her frequent reasons for dissatisfaction and distress.

It was now the gloomy month of November, a period rendered still more dreary in these parts by the early commencement of a winter seven months in its duration. I well remember it was the 10th day of the month, and I was seated in my little parlour, ruminating on the dreary prospect before me, when the father of the girl—who, by the way, was now a matron, having been married some half-score of years, and given birth to several children—entered the room unexpectedly, habited in the guise of an Indian. I was struck with the fearful distortion of his countenance, in which the worst passions of rage and revenge were depicted. My first impulse on witnessing the unusual spectacle, was a feeling that he meditated some evil design upon myself; but a moment's reflection convinced me that the supposition was fallacious, for his family had been invariably treated by me with great kindness, and he himself, notwithstanding the evil character that he bore, was personally indebted to me in many important respects. I therefore fixed my eye upon him, and calmly awaited till he should break the moody silence which prevailed, and explain the object of his visit. This he presently did, informing me in a sullen tone, that he had come to request my permission to proceed in quest of his daughter, who, he said, had recently eloped from her husband; adding his determination that she should not survive the disgrace which she had thus brought, not only upon herself, but upon every member of the family.

Knowing well the stern and revengeful character of the man with whom I had to deal, I endeavoured to calm his fury, by representing the heinousness of the crime he evidently meditated; resolving at the same time to watch his motions narrowly, lest, in his thirst for blood, some other most innocent victim might fall a sacrifice. On inquiring more particularly, I learned that the unfortunate woman was residing with her Indian paramour at a neighbouring village; but seeing the state of mind in which the father was, I conceived it prudent to refuse him the permission he so earnestly solicited. Upon this he declared his intention of sending his sons for her, since on no account should she reside longer with the partner of her infidelity. To this arrangement I could, of course, make no objection, and accordingly could only renew my determination to watch the father closely, and to interfere at once if I perceived any open manifestation of the sinister designs he had cherished, but which, I was fain to hope, the delay that would take place, and the influence of my reasonings, would have the effect of counteracting. I felt relieved when my uncouth visitor had departed, for his features, naturally saturnine and forbidding, were now distorted by an expression perfectly demoniacal.

Shortly after his departure, the poor mother made her appearance, and with tears implored me to restrain her husband's fury. I could only assure her of my determination not to permit him to proceed to any extreme measures, and this, I was happy to observe, had the effect of tranquillizing her fears in some measure.

The sons set out so secretly that no one was aware of their departure until some time afterwards. Meanwhile, as we well knew that, dead or alive, they would not return without their frail and disgraced sister, both the mother and myself employed our influence, in order to prepare the father for the trying interview that awaited him. It was not till after the lapse of fifteen days that the young men returned, bringing with them the now penitent woman. She was received by her mother in the most affectionate manner, only the gentlest reproaches for the misery which her misconduct had occasioned, being mingled with her abundant tears. As for the father, he kept aloof in gloomy impatience of a scene so affecting to others, and on his daughter's approaching to implore his forgiveness, he spurned her from him, and turning about, walked moodily to his dwelling. The daughter, who had fallen into violent hysterics, was carried in after him; and while in this state, I besought the father to compassionate the penitence she so obviously manifested. Not obtaining a reply to my satisfaction, and dreading no serious consequences, while supposing that natural affection would soon resume its sway, I left the scene, and returned home.

Under pretext of holding a consultation with his Indian relatives, the father next day summoned them to meet him.

When they were assembled at the spot he had designated—a small green in the neighbourhood—the old man, followed by the majority of his family, not excepting the subject of his appeal, presently made his appearance. The principal individual of the group, the unhappy victim of a pernicious education, stood, with downcast air, on the left: but her grief had greatly subsided, and she was now more calm than when I last saw her. Doubtless she hoped that, the cup of her affliction being now full to the brim, forgiveness on the part of her father would ensue. Alas! how mistaken were her anticipations, how erroneous the hopes we had all entertained up to this moment!

The scene was of brief duration; the words spoken, few and dreadful in their import. Every one kept silence, and the eyes of many were turned wistfully upon that relentless old man. At length the oppressive silence was broken.

"My daughter," said he, "has brought shame upon me: it is thus I efface the stain."

With this, he sprang suddenly towards her; and, ere a hand could move to arrest his purpose, or a tongue could utter one word to divert it, he plunged his dagger in her heart. Then, instantaneously disengaging it, he repeated the blow on his own bosom, and both fell lifeless on the ground.

The consternation to which this tragic catastrophe gave rise, had not yet subsided, when a man dressed like a traveller, and whom I recognized as the husband of the unfortunate woman, appeared suddenly among the assembled crowd. He bore a bloody dagger in his hand, and with a loud voice proclaimed the death of the paramour of his faithless wife.

"He no longer survives my disgrace," said he, "and I am now contented."

With these words he disappeared, and I never afterwards fell in with him.

I shall not attempt to describe the grief of the survivors of this wretched family; how the mother swooned at the unexpected termination of the meeting, and how the other members of the family deplored in turn the death of a father and a sister. Suffice it to say that, in common with others, tears flowed freely from my own eyes, as I surveyed the dismal scene, and witnessed the harrowing lamentations of the assembled mourners.

Years have elapsed since the occurrences above related took place. Still, day after day, does the disconsolate widow continue to visit the joint grave, in which, by her own desire, the remains of her husband and daughter were deposited. There, seated in silent grief, does she mourn their fate, bedewing with tears the lonely spot they occupy, while deploring incessantly the sad and mournful event of which I have constituted myself the chronicler.*

* The custom of thus mourning over the last resting place of the dead, is prevalent among most of the tribes west of the Rocky Mountains. Their expressions of grief, however, are generally exceedingly vociferous; save when the silent tear drops unseen, in unfeigned sorrow, upon the grave of some beloved object.

PLATE VI.

Prayer for the Success of the Hunt

CHAPTER XII.

The Shewappe Murder

IN a former sketch, I endeavoured to impress upon my readers the extent to which the Indian character has been misunderstood, and how greatly misrepresented, by writers not duly qualified by actual residence among these wild races, to form a just opinion concerning them. It is idle to suppose that the casual visitor who may chance to penetrate as far as the confines of our *terra incognita,* can have any real knowledge of the passions which agitate the savage breast. After getting a sly peep at some half-score of ragamuffins, and being perchance humbugged with a well-conned routine of hypocritical pretence on their part, such an one may indeed return home, deeming himself become, as if by magic, quite an oracle on the subject, but how greatly he may deceive himself, and how little he may know of their evil propensities, let these pages testify. To be brief, every Indian is not a hero, nor every female a Penelope, as some would fain insist; and in proof that they can be both ungrateful and treacherous, let me adduce the following recent and dreadful example.

B—— was one of my oldest and worthiest friends. Our intimacy had commenced some twenty-five years ago, and been ripened by time into the warmest friendship. We had shared in each other's perils; and the narrow escapes we had so frequently experienced, tended to draw still more closely the bond of amity by which we were united. It was our custom to contrive an annual meeting, in order that we might pass a few weeks in each other's company. This *reunion* naturally possessed charms for both of us; for it was a source of mixed joy, to fight like old soldiers "our battles o'er again," over a choice bottle of Port or Madeira; to lay our plans for the future, and, like veritable gossips, to propose fifty projects, not one of which there was any intention on either part to realize.

In anticipation of our customary meeting, I was occupied early in the spring of the last year, in making my preparations for setting out, as soon as the breaking up of the season should permit; ruminating, while thus engaged, on the pleasure that awaited me, and thinking it a weary while till the short month that intervened before I could leave my post should set me at liberty. Under these circumstances, one day, notice was brought that a messenger, apparently an European, and from the direction in which he approached, evidently from the lower frontier, was seen hastily making his way across the lake which lay before my establishment, and which presented at the season an unbroken surface of ice thickly covered with a dazzling bed of snow. He proved to be one of our best pedestrians from the quarter we supposed, striding with laborious perseverance through the snow, in which, notwithstanding his huge snow-shoes, he sunk deep at every step. At length, he reached the hill upon which I was standing; and handing his packet to me, said abruptly,—

"Monsieur B——— is no more; he was murdered by ———," naming the Indian by whom the dreadful deed had been committed, and who was well known to me. After recovering in some measure from the grief and surprise into which the abrupt communication of the sad intelligence had thrown me, I returned to the house, and sat down to peruse the letters I had received, from which I gathered the following particulars.

One of the Shewappe chiefs, who, from the modest and peaceful demeanour he usually exhibited, had received among us the surname of *Le Tranquille*, had after a protracted illness, recently died. The last act of his life fully justified the complimentary epithet by which we had distinguished him. Fearing that his relations might be tempted to commit some act of revenge upon an innocent victim, in their grief for his death, he especially enjoined them to refrain from any act of this nature. He insisted more particularly on their not molesting the whites, to whose constant kindness and humanity he confessed his obligation.

"Go, however," said he, "to the Chief, Mr. B——, and ask him, on my part, for a blanket, wherein to shroud all that will remain of me."

These were nearly the poor sufferer's last words; for he shortly afterwards gave up the ghost. One of the sons upon this immediately set out, bearing his father's last message to the fort; but the widow, whose grief had at first restrained her sterner feelings, soon burst forth in an ecstasy of frantic passion. Seizing a gun, which had once belonged to him who now lay lifeless before her, she exclaimed with energy—

"With this must my husband's death be revenged, and that ere another sun shall have run his course. Go, my son," she continued, turning to the eldest boy who stood weeping near her, "go, and revenge your father, whose death the foul machinations of others have occasioned, and whom you now, like a child, stand idly lamenting. Go, go!" she impetuously added, seeing that her remonstrances had as yet produced but little effect; "go, and let the victim you select be of no ordinary rank."

The better feelings of the young man, it is but fair to remark, long sustained him under the virulent reproaches with which his infuriated mother sought to urge him to this crime. Indeed, her reiterated abuse so affected his spirits, that he sought to commit suicide rather than endure her gibes and provocations any longer. At length, frustrated in the attempt upon his own life, and driven to desperation when twitted with the cowardice of a woman, and with other opprobrious epithets, by his unfeeling mother, he seized the gun, and set out on his way to the fort, resolved to glut his angry feelings by the murder of my unfortunate friend.

Meanwhile the younger brother had reached the house, and recounting his melancholy story, had received not only the blanket requested by his dying father, but a further present, which B——'s friendship for the defunct had prompted him to make. Pleased with the result of his mission, and breathing thanks to his friendly host, the young Indian set out on his return to the lodge. It may be that his solitary path on the way home was crossed by the intended murderer of his benefactor.

Poor B—— was walking to and fro in a spacious hall, in which it was customary to receive the Indian visitors at the establishment, when a young man, whom he easily recognized as the eldest son of *Tranquille* entered, and complaining of the cold (for it was midwinter) seated himself shivering by the fireside. After smoking and talking for some time on divers topics, my unfortunate friend turned with the view of entering an adjoining chamber, when his companion levelled his gun, and fired the contents, consisting of a bullet with a quantity of shot, full into his back. His victim fell without a groan, and the conscience-stricken murderer, before the alarm could be spread, was already out of reach, fleeing madly to a distance in search of that safety which he well knew he had compromised by this ruthless deed.

Thus perished my old companion, with whom, for so many years, I had been united in the strictest bonds of friendship. Thus without the interval of even a moment, after the death blow was dealt, was his spirit ushered into the presence of that dread Being before whose tribunal—a just, but yet a merciful one—we must one day all appear. What my feelings on this sad occasion must have been, I shall not attempt to describe; the lapse of time has only alleviated the poignancy of my grief, and I am now resigned to the hope, that when a dark futurity shall no longer be to me as "future," I may meet my friend in another and a better world, where ruthless revenge, and every darker passion of our nature, shall be unknown.

The sequel of this sad history I shall dismiss with brevity; for why dwell particularly upon the retributive measures which the paramount necessity of securing ourselves from the like attacks, compelled us to adopt. After many fruitless attempts, the murderer was at length secured: not without the co-operation of the natives themselves, who when they found us bent upon enforcing justice, began one by one to abandon the culprit, whom they were at first inclined to protect, but now, with their usual fickleness, did not hesitate to betray. His person at last being secured, Mr. C——, the leader of the party which had effected the capture, was desirous of taking him to the fort, there to be publicly hanged as an example *in terrorem* to the rest. The project, however, was frustrated in the following manner:—

As it was necessary to cross the river, the prisoner was placed in a canoe, with two guards, having his hands manacled. By violent exertions, the unhappy man, now rendered desperate, contrived to upset the canoe when in mid-channel, and fettered as he was, succeeded in reaching the shore. A shot from one of his countrymen now compelled him to betake himself to the water again, and, strange to relate, he recrossed the river. A second wound drove him once more towards the middle of the stream, when seeing that there was no longer the shadow of a chance of escape, and bleeding profusely from the wounds he had received, he raised himself for a moment in the water, called out, in a loud voice, acknowledging the justice of his punishment, and then sank to rise no more.

CHAPTER XIII.

The Storm.—
The Mother's Grave

MANY years have passed away since an apparent accident made me the witness of an affecting scene, the impression of which time has not even yet effaced from my memory. I was at the time on a visit to Canada. Our route lay through Lake Superior, the largest sheet of water in North America, and but too well known to the voyager for the many dangers that attend its navigation. On the occasion to which I allude, we had indeed a very narrow escape from destruction. During the early part of the day a favourable breeze had driven us rapidly forward on our course; but towards the afternoon the gathering clouds, and other well-known signs, gave indications of an approaching storm. Presently the wind began to increase till it blew a gale; loud claps of thunder pealed overhead, and echoed along the mountainous shores of the lake, while rain-drops large and heavy began to fall fast upon us. Naturally a timid sailor, I had some time before given directions to shorten sail; the prudence of which was now evident, insomuch that the crew began to see the extent of the danger which hitherto, with their usual supineness, they had not recognized. The bold rocky shores by which we were fast driving precluded the possibility of a landing; indeed any attempt to approach for such a purpose, with our frail canoe, would have been to court inevitable destruction. As the storm increased, so did the apprehensions of the majority of the crew multiply; but fortunately the two *boutes*, to whose experienced care the management of the vessel was confided, retained their self-possession, and while the rest were devoutly crossing themselves, and invoking the name of their patron saint, these wrought hard for the common safety. For myself the while, I will confess that, while I retained my outward self-possession, my hope of escape was but slender.

After scudding along for some time, a low point appeared at the distance of several miles in advance. To attain this was now our object. Hope began to revive in the minds of the despairing crew, who had for some time been in dread of sharing the fate of some of their companions, who had perished under similar circumstances, in this very neighbourhood, the preceding year. Kettles were now employed to keep the canoe clear of water by baling; paddles to assist the impulse of the shortened sail; and thus, after nearly an hour of anxious expectation, we reached the promised haven in safety. Rounding the point, we found ourselves suddenly in smooth water, sheltered from the wind, which still continued to blow with violence.

By means of my gun, which I had succeeded in keeping dry while everything else in the canoe was soaking, we made a fire; the tent was then pitched, and the crew found instant provision for their comfort by turning the canoe upon its side before the blazing faggots.

By-and-by, the storm subsided, and I sauntered abroad. Looking towards the end of the bay, I perceived, what had not before attracted my attention, a thin smoke arising from among the trees. Approaching the spot, I discovered a small encampment, but it was tenantless; and I was conjecturing what had become of its recent occupants, when my ear was caught by a low moaning sound in the vicinity. Directing my steps towards the spot, I saw, in the midst of a small clearance, a newly-covered grave, at the head of which a rude cross was planted. Near it was seated a middle-aged Indian, having in his arms a young infant, whose lips he strained to his breast—if haply he might quiet it with the fallacious hope of that nutriment of which the death of its mother, who evidently lay interred before them, had deprived it. Another child, a girl of five years old, lay at his feet weeping bitterly. He, too, the father of these little ones, by the half-suppressed moans which from time to time escaped him, gave token of the deep grief which oppressed his soul.

After witnessing for a while this moving scene, I drew near, and the noise of my approach attracted his attention. I saluted him, and he quietly rose to accept my proffered hand. With the few words of the Sautean language I possessed, I then invited him to our camp. He followed me in silence, carrying tenderly his half-dying infant, and followed by the little girl, whose grief was hushed for a season by the novelty of my unexpected visit.

The hunger of the infant was soon appeased with a little white sugar tied in linen. We also supplied its fond parent and his other little one with food, and after a time, while enjoying the solace of a pipe of tobacco, he told me his brief history. Deprived of his wife by sickness, who had died in the neighbouring camp only the day before, he had just rendered the last sad offices to her remains when I arrived, and there found him, as I have related, in the indulgence of that grief which, stoic though he is supposed by hasty and ill-informed observers to be, is no less characteristic of the American savage, than of the civilized European. Our unexpected visit diverted the grief of the poor savage. We supplied him with tobacco and ammunition, the first as a luxury, the last to procure food, and next day took our departure; our Indian friend setting out at the same time in the opposite direction, in quest of a camp of his relations who were at some distance beyond, upon the shores of the lake. Fine weather and a pleasant breeze advanced us rapidly on our journey, and we soon forgot the dangers of Lake Superior, though not the little incident which I have endeavoured to place on record.

CHAPTER XIV.

The Suicide's Cross

A FEW days after my arrival at the post last mentioned, while anxiously awaiting the friends whom I expected to accompany me on my journey, I was strolling idly about the vicinity, and had not wandered far from the house, when I was surprised at beholding a solitary cross, standing in the middle of a small secluded plain.

This emblem of Christianity, under any circumstances, possesses for me, as I fancy for most others, a peculiar attraction; and in the present instance I felt singularly disposed to inquire the reason of its being placed in a spot so remote from the ordinary place of interment. In most cases, a rude wooden crucifix indicates the last resting-place of the *voyageur*, but this which I now saw was so situated as rather to suggest that it had been placed there by some good Christian to mark the retreat where he might recite in solitude his daily orisons. The following day I renewed my visit to the spot, accompanied by my kind host and his lady, when, in answer to my inquiries, I received the following account of the object that had awakened my curiosity.

The cross, contrary to the conclusion I had arrived at, marked but too truly the resting-place of a fellow-creature, and had been erected some two months before, over the remains of an unfortunate being who had here voluntarily terminated his existence. Too weak to bear the reverses which sooner or later must always overtake the infatuated gamester, the unhappy man had dared to rush unbidden into eternity, adding one more to the long list of victims to the fatal propensity that had for some time spread but too securely its toils around him.

How deceitful are appearances! A few short years before the sad catastrophe, this young man had been selected by Mr. D——, a Roman Catholic missionary, on one of his visits to this neighbourhood, as a fit subject for religious improvement. Such was the favourable impression made by his external appearance upon the mind of the worthy priest, that the latter took him zealously by the hand. The assiduity and apparent devotion displayed in his conduct confirmed these prepossessions, and in addition to the pains taken to instruct him in the observance of the faith of which he shortly became a confirmed professor, many little acts of favour and attention, in the shape of presents and the like, marked the degree of favour to which he had attained.

But alas! the seeds of religion had been sown on a sandy soil, and as they sprang up quickly, so they grew rank, and perished! To be candid, moreover, a wearisome routine of prayers, only half intelligible, and repeated by rote without that internal impulse which renders prayer efficacious, is but a poor protection against the allurements and temptations of the world. Such proved to be the case in the present instance. Trials arose, and the unfortunate lad fell, like other worldlings, a victim to temptation, unrestrained by religious principle.

The career of a gambler is too much the same under all circumstances to require much elucidation. A few years ago I had seen the unhappy subject of my story in the bloom of early manhood, occupying a respectable situation, and respected by all around him. A year before his death I had again seen him, but how great was the contrast. Haggard, and with downcast eyes, he was squatted with scarce a garment to cover him, in the corner of the lodge; shunned by lukewarm relations, and the friends of his more prosperous days,—those hollow friends who had themselves assisted in his ruin; no one save his aged mother seemed to retain the least regard for the ill-fated gamester. What wonder is it, under these circumstances, that despair should obtain the mastery over a spirit so broken, and a resolution so weak as his! One Sabbath morning, when all the other inmates of the lodge, with the neighbours who resided around, were assembled at mass, the long-desired opportunity presented itself. His poor mother returned, and where she had left her son, there met her eyes the shattered remains of a suicide! Whether to mark their abhorrence of the crime, or from a reluctance to associate, even in death, with the Protestants, who chiefly used the ordinary burial-place, I know not; but his relatives preferred interring him close by the spot where the crime was committed. There stood, and I doubt not stands at this hour, as a memorial of the unhappy dead, the Suicide's Cross.

CHAPTER XV.

Death of our Favourite Donkey

AMONG the many losses arising from the severity of the winter, to us the unkindest cut of all was the death of an ass, which had attained the patriarchal age of thirty years, and has left behind him a numerous progeny to bear testimony to his manifold good qualities. Surely his sad end ought to be recorded, if it were only to show that the most harmless and helpless of all creatures have no security against the murderous intentions of the Indians, in these wilds!

Feeling the cold like his neighbours, and trusting to the hospitality of man, the confiding animal had approached the hut of an Indian resident in the neighbourhood, with the view of obtaining a little warmth from the fire. Aged, and withal tired, perhaps, a deep sleep had succeeded to this unwonted luxury, and while thus napping, the poor brute was treacherously assailed with axe and knife, by those who should have protected him, as their guest. That "murder will out" is a proverb as old as the hills. It was not long ere many-tongued rumour let the secret escape, nor was much time suffered to elapse before the hue-and-cry was raised, and the criminals brought before the presiding judge, their hands still red with the blood of their victim. The culprits were about to be questioned on the ruthless deed, when a voice was heard calling out to give them the benefit of "Lynch law." The judge signified his disapprobation of this violation of propriety, by ordering the court to be cleared, and presently, considering the highly excited state of public feeling, resolved to defer the examination until it should in some degree have subsided: for who, whether beast or man, was ever of sufficient importance to be long regretted?

After six days' confinement, the trial was resumed. It was of short duration: the facts being too obvious to admit of question. When called upon for their defence, the prisoners pleaded starvation as their motive; but this no one chose to credit. The man then laid the blame upon his wife, or the devil—one or the other of whom he declared to have instigated the deed. This dastardly attempt to shift the blame upon his unfortunate partner, occasioned a murmur of disapprobation, which the judge was compelled to check in a peremptory tone. It was then proved that the prisoners had hitherto sustained a good reputation for industry and good behaviour, a fact which evidently had its weight with the jury. At length the judge, whose well-known character for discretion I need not comment upon, charged the jury, warning them to dismiss all prejudice from their minds, and so forth, and they retired to deliberate. After a few minutes, a verdict of guilty was returned, accompanied by a recommendation to mercy, on the score of ignorance of the enormity of their crime. The sentence passed upon the prisoners was—banishment for ever from the county of Vancouver.

Such a punishment may at first sight appear lenient; but its severity will become apparent, when it is understood that death itself is perhaps less insupportable to the Indian, than banishment from his native soil. It is the pride and the pleasure of his nature to speak of it. Every conspicuous spot has its appropriate name, possibly connected by tradition with the prowess of his departed ancestors. When a distant journey is undertaken, the last recommendation to those he leaves behind, is, "Fail not, in case of my death, to go in quest of my bones, and bring them to my own lands." I have witnessed several instances of Indians dying in this way, not less than twenty days' journey from their ancestral home; still, through a country nearly impassable, have the relatives observed religiously that last injunction, and sought their remains, exposed to every manner of privations and hardship. This being well known, ought we not to feel commiseration for the unfortunates, whom we so often see deprived of their natural rights, particularly in the United States, where, with the regularity of a law of nature, the aboriginal inhabitants are compelled to recede before the white population? As the settlements advance with rapid strides, a questionable remuneration, it is true, is nominally made to the original possessors of the soil, but what compensation can remunerate even these poor outcasts for the violation of their dearest sympathies? Driven backwards, step by step, and league by league, each stage of their retreat is but a temporary respite from the onward march which dooms them to die at a distance from the bones of their forefathers. Wretched and desponding—moved hither and thither, by the right of might—subject to the will of a coarse and unfeeling agent, acting in the name of a government which it is hopeless to resist— they become a prey to contagious diseases, which are ever severest on the poor and miserable. It is almost the only consolation remaining to the philanthropist under these circumstances, that, ere long, the race must become extinct.

In the Oregon territory, the population was once numerous, as compared with the ordinary population of America. But disease has done its work there also, insomuch that scarcely one of the original race is now to be seen. Well do I recollect the day, when the banks of the Columbia and its tributaries were crowded by hundreds of the native races, apparently among the happiest of mankind, and surrounded by abundance, which it cost them little labour to procure. The river supplied them with salmon, the woods yielded elk and deer, and where wood was scarce, in the upper parts of the watercourse, an adequate supply of fuel was brought down by the annual floods from the mountains. But how is the scene changed! Immigration has supplanted the original population of the land, and where peace and contentment once reigned, they reign no longer.

CHAPTER XVI.

The London Packet

IT is not easy for me to convey an idea of the degree of excitement that attends the glad announcement of the packet from London. Shut out from the world, indeed, as we are, and receiving tidings from home at yearly intervals only, it is natural that anxiety as to their probable nature should prevail among the expectants. Such being the case, it is also always interesting to observe the varied manifestations of joy or grief, that are exhibited by individuals according to the intelligence received by them.

For weeks before the anticipated event, the probabilities attending it form the all-pervading topic of conversation, both among the private circles and at the public mess of our little community. A thousand conjectures arise in quick succession to divide the opinions of those interested, & these are often strengthened by bets upon the points in debate. The excitement increases from day to day, until all doubts are at length solved by the arrival of the ship, first announced by a confused murmur, and then by the noisy exclamations of the children, running to and fro, delighted with the novelty, and screaming at the top of their voices, "The Packet! the Packet!"

The bearers of the precious burden shortly make their appearance, not a little proud of the temporary importance attached to their mission. They advance to the governor's domicile, and are ushered into the presence hall, where, as they well know, a hearty welcome from the great man awaits them. All etiquette is for the while suspended. A motley group of followers throng around the doors. A few brief inquiries as to the whereabouts of the good ship, and the like generalities, terminate the first act of the important drama, and the packet-bearers are dismissed kitchenwards, where refreshments await them, and their share of the matter is concluded.

Deeply impressed with the importance of his office, the accountant, who, in these matters seems privileged to take the lead, now advances, & hastily rummages through the contents of the box. Letters are doled forth to their expectant owners. The man of figures seizes with avidity the mass of accounts and books, which seem to possess for him attractions not easily appreciated by the uninitiated, and forthwith retreats to his desk, where he plunges deep into their mysteries, and seems for the while weaned from extraneous cares.

As may be supposed, an event so long looked for, and so interesting to all connected with the establishment, deranges for a while its settled routine; every one, in short, being so engrossed with the perusal of his letters, that a general silence supplants the ordinary buzz of business. At length, the sound of the dinner-bell renews the social compact, the contents of each one's budget are retailed for the general benefit, an extra glass of wine is drunk in honour of the day, and joy and hilarity, with occasional exceptions, are exhibited in every countenance. Even the ladies share in the general excitement; for besides the familiar topics in which they may be presumed to have an interest, they have their own special curiosity to satisfy, noting the domestic supplies shipped for them — the gowns, the bonnets, the shawls, and fifty other items of necessity or ornament. So passes the day; another sun appears, and again all is regularity and order.

I well remember a scene such as I have described in June 18—. Among those assembled at the dinner-table on this occasion, I remarked one young man, recently from England, in the capacity of a clerk, whose thoughtful look excited my sympathy. I afterwards learned that he had received no letters from home, which accounted in some degree for the sad expression of his countenance. He was the only son of a widow, and beside her he had no other tie upon earth, for every relative he had ever known, had one by one been snatched from his side. The disappointment he had experienced was indeed great, but I had no suspicion that the wound it had inflicted was so serious, until his absence from breakfast the next morning suggesting the propriety of calling upon him, I found him bathed in tears, and having comforted him as well as I could, left him once more to his meditations.

The poor fellow had imbibed the idea, afterwards proved to be erroneous, that his sole relation was dead, for to no other cause could he ascribe her unaccountable silence; and it was in vain that we pointed out to him the possibility of her letters having miscarried.

Thus, from hour to hour, did the lad pine away, secretly indulging the gloomy imaginings which it was soon evident would sap the foundations of his health. The pallor of death began to supplant the rosy hue which his countenance had previously exhibited. Medical advice was resorted to, but his disease was of the mind, and beyond the help of medicine.

Day after day he got worse, and within a brief fortnight after the arrival of the packet, he expired, a victim to over-excitement and despair!